MUSEUM of AMERICAN FINANCE

AUTOMOTIVE GIANTS
OF AMERICA

Men Who Are Making Our Motor Industry

BY
B. C. FORBES
AND
O. D. FOSTER

B. C. FORBES PUBLISHING CO.
120 FIFTH AVENUE, NEW YORK

COPYRIGHT, 1926, BY
THE B. C. FORBES PUBLISHING CO.

THE PLIMPTON PRESS
NORWOOD · MASS · U·S·A

CONTENTS

	PAGE
Harry H. Bassett	1
Roy D. Chapin	14
Walter P. Chrysler	30
William C. Durant	44
Albert R. Erskine	61
Harvey S. Firestone	77
Henry Ford	94
Charles D. Hastings	110
Frederick J. Haynes	121
John Hertz	141
Edward S. Jordan	155
Charles F. Kettering	169
Alvan Macauley	178
Charles S. Mott	193
Charles W. Nash	211
R. E. Olds	225
Alfred P. Sloan, Jr.	237
H. H. Timken	252
Walter C. White	265
John N. Willys	279

INTRODUCTION

CURIOUSLY, although our automobile industry is young, its leaders are not young men. The average age of the twenty foremost is a shade under fifty-five. Only three of them are in the forties.

Every one of the twenty is self-made. Most of them had only a moderate amount of schooling. Nine had some college training.

Few of them started life in any mechanical or engineering line of work. Office boys lead. Grocery boys and farm boys are well represented.

Not one of the twenty comes from the Far-West. The East and the Middle-West gave birth to most of them, although the South can claim three. Ohio produced four, New York three and Michigan three. Only one was not born in America, a record probably not matched by any other industry of first importance.

The following table gives the name, the birthplace, the age, the first job and the schooling of each of the twenty whose careers are narrated in this book:

INTRODUCTION

Name	Birthplace	Age 1926	First Job	Education
Harry Bassett	Utica, N.Y.	51	Office Boy	High School Graduate
Roy D. Chapin	Lansing, Mich.	46	Auto-Demonstrator	Univ. of Mich.
Walter P. Chrysler	Wamego, Kansas	51	Grocery Store	Public School
William C. Durant	Boston, Mass.	65	Grocery Store	Public School
Albert R. Erskine	Huntsville, Ala.	55	Office Boy	Public School
Harvey S. Firestone	Columbiana Co., Ohio	58	Travelling Salesman	High School and Business College
Henry Ford	Dearborn, Mich.	63	Farm Work	Public School
Charles D. Hastings	Hillsdale, Mich.	68	Newspaper Route	High School Graduate
Frederick J. Haynes	Cooperstown, N.Y.	55	Grocery Store	Mech. Eng., Cornell, one year
John Hertz	Austria	46	Office Boy	Public School
Edward S. Jordan	Merrill, Wis.	44	Newspaper Boy	Graduate, Univ. of Wis.
Charles F. Kettering	Ashland Co., Ohio	52	Country School-teacher	Ohio State Univ.
Alvan Macauley	Wheeling, W. Va.	54	Patent Attorney's Office	Lehigh and George Wash. Univs.
Charles S. Mott	Newark, N.J.	51	Factory	Stevens Institute
Charles W. Nash	DeKalb, Ill.	62	Farm Boy	Public School
R. E. Olds	Geneva, Ohio	62	Father's Shop	High School Graduate
Alfred P. Sloan, Jr.	New Haven, Conn.	51	Draughtsman	Graduate, Mass. Inst. of Tech.
H. H. Timken	St. Louis, Mo.	58	Order Clerk	Graduate, Law School
Walter C. White	Cleveland, Ohio	50	Law Office	Cornell
John N. Willys	Canandaigua, N.Y.	53	Laundry	Public School

INTRODUCTION

No other industry in this country or anywhere else in the world ever enjoyed such growth or accomplished so much in the brief space of twenty-five years.

America's automotive industry employs 3,200,000 workers. Its assets approximate $2,000,000,000. The 1925 production reached $3,000,000,000 in value. Automotive exports exceeded $1,000,000 every day of the year, a total of 550,000 vehicles being exported for the year; last year, reports the Government, " automotive products in export trade exceeded any other fabricated product, and their position was third among exported products of all kinds, being exceeded only by unmanufactured cotton and refined mineral oils."

In 1925 there were produced, according to the records compiled by the National Automobile Chamber of Commerce, 3,833,000 cars and 482,000 trucks, valued (wholesale) at $2,500,000,000 and $500,000,000. The year's output of 55,750,000 tires was valued at $886,700,000. In addition, parts and accessories were consumed to the amount of $1,000,000,000.

The average retail price of the 1925 cars was $866 and of trucks $1,350.

The total number of motor vehicles registered in the United States approximates 20,000,000 — 17,500,000 cars and 2,500,000 trucks. The rest of the world shows only 4,600,000 motor vehicles registered — which is exactly the number registered on U. S. farms alone.

There are in this country more than 47,000 car and truck dealers, 55,000 public garages, 75,000 service stations and repair shops, 61,000 supply stores.

The industry in 1925 called for 3,040,000 railway cars to make its shipments. Of all the rubber consumed in the United States, the automobile industry uses 84 per cent. It utilizes half of our total plate glass production, 11 per cent. of our iron and steel production, 65 per cent. of our upholstery leather. Crude rubber used in manufacturing tires in 1925 totalled 769,000,000 pounds and cotton fabric 226,000,000 pounds.

Think of it: one family in every eight families in the United States derive their livelihood from the automotive industry.

America could not have attained such a dominating position in the greatest industry created during the twentieth century had not many of our best brains been attracted to it and devoted wholeheartedly to it. Our automotive giants are essentially men of courage, men of initiative, men of vision. How else could there have been created productive capacity of over 5,000,000 vehicles a year, when year after year from the very start there have been direful prophesies of impending " saturation," of impending disaster?

How the foremost leaders have brought the automotive industry to its unique eminence is told in the following sketches, all of which have appeared in *Forbes Magazine*, half of them written by O. D. Foster and half by the writer.

B. C. FORBES

HARRY H. BASSETT

THE place of honor at the Annual Automobile Show in New York has been won year after year by Buick. Its sales have regularly ranked first among all exhibitors.

What accounts for such a record?

Who, rather, is responsible for it?

Behind Buick is, of course, the greatest automobile organization in the world, General Motors, with its unmatched corps of research engineers, inventors and chemists, its unlimited financial resources, its brainy executives and organizers.

But behind nearly every conspicuously successful business enterprise there is one man. So is it with Buick.

That man is Harry H. Bassett.

How does he operate?

First, by constantly improving the product; and

Second, by winning the cordial co-operation of all ranks of workers as well as the dealers.

And the second is probably the more important.

An illustration: It came to his ears one day that the men in a certain department were grumbling, that they felt they were not being fairly paid. Harry Bassett didn't delegate any third party to ferret out who was causing the trouble, nor did he call anyone on the carpet. He sauntered into the department, just as he constantly informally visits all departments. He turned a box on end, stood up on it, and waved to the men to gather around.

"What's the trouble boys? I hear you're not satisfied. Tell me all about it and let's see if we can't straighten it out right away."

The men looked at one another and several beckoned to a certain man to do the talking.

"We're not earning enough, Harry," the workman spoke up. "It isn't that we're not satisfied with the rate, but there isn't enough work coming through to give us a chance to make good pay."

After getting the exact facts, Bassett told them: "I think you're right. The rate is fair enough, as you admit, but I see that we are not giving you enough production. By the fifteenth of next month enough work should be coming along to keep you all busy so that you can make good money. It isn't your fault that there isn't enough coming along just now to keep you going full tilt; it's our fault. I'll tell you what we'll do. We'll make good the shortage between now and the fifteenth. After that I'm sure you will all be satisfied."

The men expressed satisfaction with this arrangement, things worked out as expected, and everybody was happy.

Here's another incident, given me by one of the Buick men when I was going over the works.

The day before Christmas Harry Bassett learned that an old machinist who had worked for the company twenty years had been stricken with an incurable sickness and was confined to his bed. A talk with the man's foreman brought out that the old man had lost his appetite and that Camembert cheese and the usual liquid accompaniment was about the only thing that appealed to him.

The president of the company, armed with a huge basket of flowers, a plentiful supply of Camembert and a still more plentiful supply of the desired liquid refreshment, visited the old machinist, whom he had worked with years before. The old man broke down completely, but it wasn't long before Harry's reminiscences, jokes and " Camembert and " had the old fellow in a genuine Christmas mood.

Harry Bassett's ideas about building up a successful automobile business differ from those of some other leaders in the industry. He doesn't believe that a product that is good enough for one year necessarily is good enough for the next year and the next.

" I believe in striving to make one's product better every year," Mr. Bassett told me. " It's important not only to make it better, but to make it look better. I have always believed that there were a sufficient number of people able and willing to pay for a car of superior design and embodying good, honest material. If you make up-to-date, attractive, honest merchandise, delivering a hundred cents' worth of genuine value for every dollar paid by the consumer, then you are in a sound economic position. Cheating, or even scrimping, doesn't go. It doesn't pay in the end."

He went on: "I always risk my own neck before we ask any purchaser to buy a car with any new device on it. For example, I thoroughly tested out four-wheel brakes on my own car before they were put on cars for the trade. Then, we had five engineers go to hot climates and cold climates and put the new brakes through all sorts of practical tests. The way to find out about a thing is to dig into it yourself and try it out yourself. Before we put anything into production at Buick, I satisfy myself by actual experience that the thing is all right by driving a car and putting the new improvement through its paces on dry roads and wet, through snow and on ice. Draughting rooms, experimental departments and all the activities of the engineers have always interested me keenly."

When a lad, Harry Bassett was ambitious to become a lawyer. How he came to enter the industrial field and how he reasoned out that the automobile industry offered the greatest possibilities is interesting.

After attending school at Utica, N. Y., where he was born on September 11, 1875, Harry was getting ready to graduate from the high school at Ilion, N. Y., when an office boy friend told him he was giving up his job and suggested that Harry apply for it. The office boy spoke to his boss, F. C. Cross, head of the Remington Arms Company, and as Mr. Cross happened to know the Bassett family, he told the boy to have Harry come and see him at once. Harry wanted the job, but he also wanted to get his high school diploma; he wanted to study law later, but did not then have the money necessary to go to college. All this he confided to Mr. Cross.

This gentleman belonged to the old school. He was stern, dignified, an excellent organizer, a strict disciplinarian.

"Young man, give up the notion of becoming a lawyer," he lectured the sixteen-year-old youth. "Within the next fifteen or twenty years industry is going to offer far greater possibilities than any profession. This country is going to see the organization of many very big companies and there will be plenty of very fine positions to be filled. Industry is only starting. Stick to it."

Harry compromised by taking the job on condition that he be allowed a day off to attend the commencement exercises and receive his certificate of graduation.

Another graduation followed rather quickly, from office boy to assistant billing clerk. Harry showed aptitude for figures, and the treasurer annexed him as his assistant.

Young Bassett had the sense to do what has landed so many men at the top of great organizations. Although engaged in office work, he diligently applied himself to familiarizing himself with factory operations. By and by he had gained such mastery of the work that he was delegated to analyze the exact cost of all sorts of factory operations so as to compile estimates for contracts. His industry was equalled by his accuracy. The company learned it could depend absolutely upon estimates drawn up by Harry Bassett.

More. His close analyses of the different operations enabled him to make suggestions for improving methods and cutting costs. He was earning his modest salary several times over.

His reward came in the form of promotion to the position of assistant general manager.

All this was not accomplished in a handclap. It cost more than twelve years of continuous, keen-eyed application to each duty that came along. He served fourteen years with the Remington Arms Company before an alert manufacturer, realizing his worth, won him away.

"I wish you would come over to the hotel and have a talk with me," was the message Bassett received one day. The visitor was Charles S. Mott, head of the Weston-Mott Company of Utica, well-known manufacturers of wire wheels and rims for bicycles, carriages and other vehicles. Mr. Mott explained that, with the advent of the automobile business, they had taken up the production of axles, hubs, and rims for automobiles and that, in order to be near the Buick Company, their largest customer, a plant was being established at Flint, Michigan. He wanted Bassett to come with his company and later go to Flint as assistant superintendent.

How did Mr. Mott know of Harry Bassett's record? He didn't know Harry Bassett; he only knew of Harry

Bassett's achievements. It had come about in this way: A wide-awake Weston-Mott salesman, Hubert Dalton, had visited Ilion many times to sell the Remington people machinery. This salesman got to know young Bassett. Bassett's attractive personality made a favorable impression. The salesman also learned of the wonderful work this young man was doing. By and by the salesman was promoted and rose to the position of superintendent of the Weston-Mott works. When expansion necessitated a plant at Flint, where he knew many factory problems would have to be met, he at once thought of Harry Bassett and urged his employer, Mr. Mott, to engage him.

"I realized," Mr. Bassett recently related, "that I had reached the cross-roads in my life. Would I stay with the Remington Arms, where I had been extremely well treated and had reached a responsible position? Or, would I accept this offer to switch into an entirely different industry?

"I took time to think it over carefully. Finally, I reached this conclusion: The rapid disappearance of forests and other game country would mean that there would be little growth in the demand for our guns. On the other hand, I sized up the new transportation vehicle, the automobile, as possessing wonderful possibilities, although at that time, 1905, the automobile was a very different product from that which it is to-day. Fortunately for me my reasoning turned out to be all right."

Bassett became assistant superintendent, first, at

Utica. Within three months Superintendent Dalton left him in charge of the entire plant and went to Flint to supervise the building of the new works. A year later Bassett went to Flint as assistant factory manager. Within twelve months he was made factory manager.

These were days of rapid expansion for the Weston-Mott Company. The automobile business was growing by leaps and bounds. Weston-Mott had to keep pace. Its products were accepted as standard.

How to find and train enough men was the most difficult problem of all. Here Harry Bassett shone. He devoted more of his time and attention to men than to machinery. He developed a notable knack for binding men to him. New workmen quickly came to look upon him more as a friend than as a boss. He thus became an extremely valuable executive. By 1913 he had become general manager, although only in his thirties. Later he was elected vice-president. But he continued to act as general manager, since this position afforded him the fullest play for his capacity for handling the now huge force of workmen.

General Motors had become by far the largest consumer of the company's products. Mr. Mott had sold a minority of his stock to General Motors, and when this concern reached the point where it was taking 60 per cent of his entire production, he agreed to exchange his Weston-Mott stock for shares in General Motors. This led to consolidation with Buick, the enterprise thus becoming easily the largest in Flint.

Young Bassett was made (in 1916) assistant general manager of the combination, which took the Buick name.

This gave him wider scope for the exercise of his talents as a handler of men. He spent precious little time in his office. He was constantly out in the factory, rubbing shoulders with the men in all departments. He was "Harry" to them. If a fellow was helping himself, he would not hesitate to offer Harry a "chew."

In less than thirty months he was made general manager, and in the following month, May, 1919, he was elected vice-president and director of the General Motors Corporation, the parent company. His aptitude for getting production was taken advantage of by putting him on the operating committee of the mammoth corporation.

In January, 1920, what was long foreseen by his associates happened: he was made president of the Buick Motor Company. And in September, 1924, he was elected a member of the executive committee of the General Motors Corporation.

Under Harry Bassett, Buick has made history. Its sales quickly topped, in dollars and cents, the sales of any other automobile company in America, with the exception of Ford, and this unique record has been maintained. In 1916, the year before Bassett first joined Buick, the total output was only 43,946 cars. By 1920, when he was made president, the production had reached 115,927 cars. Three years later the extraordinary total of 201,975 was reached.

Harry Bassett would be the last man to claim any great share of the credit for Buick's phenomenal success. If you were to suggest that he had done wonders, he would immediately tell you that you were mistaken, that most of the credit really belonged to others. He would tell you how much Buick as well as other General Motor companies owed to the business statesmanship of Pierre duPont, to the farsighted co-operation of President A. P. Sloan of General Motors (with whom he did business back in the days when Sloan was with the Hyatt Roller Bearing Company), to his close friend and former employer, C. S. Mott, and to " all the other boys in the plant."

But every one of these men would, in turn, tell you how important has been the part played by Harry Bassett in the upbuilding of the Buick company. His forte is not finance, but factory operation. He is never satisfied to let things move along in a rut. "We must improve it," he constantly urges. A design that was successful this year is not one to be retained next year if the most diligent effort can produce something better. Since progress is the law of the world, Bassett insists that it must be the law with Buick.

How well this principle has worked can be gathered from the fact that, compared with sales to wholesalers in 1915 of $46,757,000, sales in 1923 reached a total of $232,136,000.

Early in 1924 it was announced that $11,000,000 was to be spent on buildings at the main Flint plant, to increase capacity to 1,200 cars a day. At the 1924

Automobile Show in New York, Mr. Bassett, in announcing the year's expansion program, said:

"Although we built more than 200,000 automobiles during the calendar year 1923, we found this record-breaking number insufficient to supply the demand for Buick cars. That demand continues, and to meet it we are considerably extending our facilities."

Much has been heard and written about the "riding" of dealers by different manufacturers. The mortality among the dealers of certain manufacturers has, indeed, been very serious. But Buick dealers stick. Harry Bassett's intense interest in men has not been confined to his "boys" at the Flint and Detroit plants. He has always had a warm spot in his heart for dealers.

"What's the use of making cars if you can't sell them?" he once said to me. "It's not enough to have your men in the factories satisfied. You must have satisfied dealers. And the only way I know of that dealers can be satisfied is to treat them right and make it possible for them to make money.

"We think we have the finest lot of dealers in the country. Why shouldn't we treat them generously? If it hadn't been for them, how could we ever have got to the top and kept at the top? They have played the game with us, and we play the game with them.

"A lot is said about 'satisfied customers.' You must satisfy your customers, of course, but that isn't enough. If you are to prosper soundly, you must lay yourself out to satisfy also the men who make your product and the men who sell your product."

After spending a day among the Buick workmen and learning how they idolized Harry Bassett, I asked him, "How do you do it?"

He replied: "Being able to get on well with men isn't a trick that somebody can teach you. Honestly, I believe that the spirit of humanness, or kindness, or whatever you want to call it, has to be born in a man. Some men simply have it. Others haven't. It so happens that I was born with a genuine feeling of — well, you might call it warmness towards my fellowmen. I like people. I like to help other fellows to get along. I get more fun out of my job than out of anything else. I know that I am very fond of all the 'boys,' and if, as you tell me, you find that some of them think that I play fair and square with them, I am gratified to know it.

"We get on all right together. The key men have been with the organization for years, all working together most harmoniously.

"You know," he added, "the policy of the General Motors Corporation tends to make a man feel satisfied and secure for the future. No corporation in America has a more generous plan for enabling its responsible men to attain a competency. Its Managers' Securities Plan makes us feel that we are working in the interest not only of the corporation but of ourselves. Under the leadership of such men as Mr. Pierre duPont and President Sloan, we are all inspired to do our level best."

After a pause, he went on: "You were talking as if

Buick's production is big and as if General Motors was an enormous corporation. Frankly, I believe that in the next ten years both will do very much bigger things than they have done in the last ten. We feel that we will be able more than to hold our own against all comers."

B. C. F.

ROY D. CHAPIN

IN THE early days of 1901 when the foreshortened Oldsmobile was still an object of wonder and envy, a young college lad slipped away from Ann Arbor in mid-semester and took the train for Detroit. Once there he lost no time making his way out to the Olds plant, and shortly he was speeding down the road with one of their engineers at the furious rate of *fifteen miles an hour*.

It was an exciting trip. He felt almost as if he were flying, and when they finally came to a stop he had both feet braced against the dashboard and was clinging to the seat. With the thrill of speed there came an enormous sense of what this new motive power was going to mean in the world of transportation.

At that moment Roy Dikeman Chapin, chairman of the Hudson Motor Car Company, chose his career. This was the coming industry. Into it he would throw every bit of energy nature had given him. He hurried into the office of Mr. Olds, who had formerly manufactured gas engines in the town of Lansing, Michigan, where Chapin was born. The factory was then just finishing its experiments and getting ready to turn out the little four and one-half horsepower, curved-dash Oldsmobile.

"I want a job in your plant," he said, his voice tense with excitement. "Can I get it?"

Mr. Olds looked at the excited boy and smiled.

"Sit down, Roy," he said kindly, "and let us talk it over."

The upshot of it was that Olds told him he was just leaving for California and would take the matter up with him when he came back, but Chapin was still insistent.

"That's a long time to wait, Mr. Olds," he persisted, "and I want to begin *now*. I don't care what you offer me so long as I can barely live on it. *I just want to be near that car.*"

More to satisfy his impetuosity than because he thought he would accept it, Mr. Olds offered him a position as demonstrator at $35 a month.

It was more than Chapin had hoped for. It meant that he would be obliged to *drive* that car, and, equally important, *ride* in it.

Nine years later that same boy was heading a company of his own which made the record first-year output of the industry at the time, with a production of 4,000 Hudson cars. It is a company which was so ably organized, so sanely managed that it has never known a setback. In 1916 it put out 26,000 of its new Super-six cars and became the largest maker of fine cars in the world. Eight years later its output ran ahead of 700 cars a day.

But in the interval there was work and plenty of it. Even young Chapin did not come into his own without all the harrowing discouragements and the hours of exhausting labor that pave the road to success.

The first few weeks sped by with amazing rapidity. He spent hours in the factory. He was at the shops early, working on some of the small parts so that he could make minor repairs. This was his first idea. Later, as his vision encompassed the limitless field he had almost unconsciously stepped into, he determined to go at it from the bottom. His whole nature rebelled at half-way measures.

He did not merely want to *drive* the car, he wanted to *make* it, and he wanted to *improve* it, to put it where it would do all the things his imagination told him it could do if it were brought to a higher state of perfection. As soon as he had mastered one of the machine tools in the shops he passed on to another. He was not satisfied until he could run them all, and before long he was deep in a study of the car's mechanical construction.

But just as he was getting to a position where his knowledge could be used to good account the factory burned down, and for a time it looked as if he would be out of a job. But the Olds Motor Works decided to rebuild, and at the same time plans were put under way for a wider distribution of the car.

Among other sales projects it was decided to start a direct-by-mail campaign which would require the use of a new and somewhat elaborate catalog. Here was Chapin's opportunity, for he was an expert photographer. In those days catalogs were not so highly illustrated as they are now. He determined to make the Olds booklet a star number.

In a corner of the reconstructed plant he built himself a dark room which was a model of convenience and utility. Here he worked without regard to hours. Finally the work was completed, and while the sales campaign was under way Chapin went back into the shops, where he proved so expert that he was appointed a tester, assisting John Maxwell, who later built the Maxwell car.

That these were indeed early days is shown by a little anecdote told me by Mr. Chapin.

"One day one of the Olds engineers and I were returning from a visit to the Wilson Body plant," said Chapin. "When we were about a mile away the steering spring broke. We worked with the thing for a while without result and then we lifted the little car around in the road and guided it back again by kicking the front wheels, my companion having assured me that in a little shop adjoining the body plant was a very clever mechanician and inventor who could fix us up.

"I was willing to be shown, but will confess that I did not feel much enthusiasm when I saw his shop, which was nothing more than a lean-to. We went in and found a slender, blue-overalled man who came out to see what was wrong with our car. As soon as he went to work I saw that he was an expert mechanician, and his interest in what he was doing was compelling.

"He bolted a plate on our broken spring and before long he had us on our way.

"As we left the shop my companion waved a farewell and called out:

"'Much obliged to you, Henry.'

"To-day that mechanician is the richest man in the world.

"It was Henry Ford."

The following summer Ford came over to the Olds plant to see how things were getting along. He was then experimenting with a heavy, phaeton type of car, and it was some time later before he built a lighter model.

Young as he is, Chapin covers in his contacts a complete directory of the automobile industry. Back in the days when the Olds plant burned, Olds was obliged for a while to purchase his materials outside. Part of his motor supplies came from Henry M. Leland, who, in the following year, headed the Cadillac company. Leland had a little shop and made beveled gears. Those were the days, too, when the Dodge brothers first made their start. At the time, they had a small machine shop down town in Detroit. Olds needed transmission gears, and started them in this line. The upholstering on the first Olds car was done by B. F. Everitt, later of Everitt-Metzger-Flanders and now president of the Rickenbacker company.

It was about this time, in the Fall of 1901, that the second auto show was to open in New York. Chapin was chosen to drive the new model of the Oldsmobile from Detroit to New York on the open road. It was the longest trip that had ever been attempted in this country with a motor car. The previous year a Winton car had been driven to the show from Cleveland, and the feat had attracted a great deal of attention.

Since there were no service stations in those days, the car had a huge box containing extra parts, bolted to the rear. The body was entirely open, and the cold was extreme. The roads, too, in many places were almost impassable. Entering Syracuse, Chapin drove along the Erie Canal tow path, bumping over the tow ropes and frightening the mules. Perhaps this experience with bad roads gave him his vision for the betterment of all American highways.

Progress was so slow that he got behind his schedule and became alarmed. Often he started out before daylight, finding it none too comfortable sliding in and out of ruts in the half-light on standard two and one-half inch single-tube tires. His first serious accident occurred when he hit a big bump at the bottom of a hill, bending an axle and losing the big box of parts. A new axle was shipped to him at Hudson, New York, where he worked well into the night installing it.

Finally, covered with dirt, grease, and the general stains of travel he reached New York City and started down Fifth Avenue to meet the Olds officials, who had preceded him by train. On the Avenue he came across one of the first motor cars he had seen since leaving Detroit, and it attracted his immediate attention. The street was slippery and the wheels of the car ahead wove in and out so strangely that he burst out laughing at the sight. At that moment some one stepped in front of his car and he hastily jammed on the brakes. The Oldsmobile turned completely around, hit the curb and broke several of the spokes in one of the wire wheels. It was a lucky escape for he was only a mile from the end of his long journey, which he completed with greater caution.

What he saw and heard at the auto show stimulated his already lively imagination. He saw movement quickened, distribution increased, transportation costs lowered, remote sections developed, all by means of this new motive power with which he was working. Distance was in a measure annihilated. Transportation was the big issue of commerce. In one way and another it was the vital factor in almost every essential of living.

More than ever he saw the big opportunities ahead for men who had the vision and initiative to grasp them. It is said that the biggest and brainiest men in the country are gathered together in automobile centers. Certain it is that the automobile industry more than any other requires vision, daring, and a quick grasp of new ideas. It has no precedents, is restricted by no hide-bound principles. Men who succeed in it must be creators, originators of new styles, new methods, new plans for mass production at minimum cost. The plants themselves, where output is large, are the acme of efficiency in construction and handling. Competition, the very soul of better output, lets no manufacturer lag along with out-of-date methods. In one way and another the automobile industry has done more than any other to put America on the map as a big producer, and to quicken her commercial activity.

With all these new ideas in his head, Chapin did not consider himself too valuable for ordinary duties, but went right back into the factory at Detroit. By this time his ability was being recognized and he was placed in charge of the repair department, now more appropriately named service department.

"What we considered an efficient service department in those days would be called a joke to-day," said Mr. Chapin. "I don't think anything would give you a better idea of the utter unreliability of the motor car at that time than the remark made by one of our owners during this very trying development period.

"Not only were we one of the first of the car manufacturers, but we were among the first to use slogans. Fred L. Smith, who was then general manager of the Olds Company and whose friendly interest and counsel was of great value to me in those early days, was the inventor of most of these slogans. One of the best of them (so we thought) was:

"'Nothing to watch but the road.'

"But it had not been out long before we heard from one of our owners.

"'The idea is good,' he said. 'But I get darned tired of watching the same piece of road.'"

Chapin's duties in the service department put him in close touch with owners of cars. He was sent all over the country and he began to develop a strong selling angle. He was quick, obliging, knew what he was talking about, and soon attracted considerable attention. At twenty-four he was made sales manager, doubtless the youngest in the industry. The Olds company at that time was the largest manufacturer of automobiles in the world.

" That statement sounds much bigger than it really was," said Mr. Chapin with a laugh. " Sales science was not so necessary in those days as a man who had confidence in the future of the car. A boy of that age who is obsessed with one idea, as I was, is bound to awaken enthusiasm, because real honest-to-goodness enthusiasm is always contagious. I did not know a thing about territorial research; sales resistance, under that name, was an unknown quantity; and statistics in the motor car field did not exist. We were pioneering, purely and simply. The world was our field, every man a prospect, and my faith in the future of the motor car never wavered for an instant. When I sold a car I sold it with the honest conviction that I was doing the buyer a favor in helping him to take his place in a big forward movement.

" However, I think I realized some of my shortcomings. At that period the National Cash Register Company had the most aggressive sales organization in industry, so I made many trips to Dayton to study their methods. Out of this experience I wrote the first sales manual used in the automobile business.

"Shortly after I went into the sales field, Howard E. Coffin was made chief engineer of the plant. It was a great step ahead for the Olds. Coffin and I were great friends and worked together very closely. From the first Coffin had a wonderful grasp of both engineering and design. Whenever he worked out something new we talked it over together both from the engineering and the sales standpoint. It helped me enormously from the sales end, and I in turn gave him any suggestions which came in to me from the selling side. Between the two of us we managed to keep pretty closely in touch with everything that was going on in the motor field."

What Mr. Chapin did not tell me, but what I learned from outside sources was that these two brilliant young men were considered, even in those days, leading lights in the automobile field. They were untiring workers. This, together with their youthful enthusiasm and a vision remarkable in those early days, marked them as future leaders in the industry.

While sales manager, Chapin had a call from a man living in Elmira, New York, who wanted to handle the Elmira agency. Later this same man, although only an agent, saved the Overland company from going into the hands of a receiver by raising enough money to keep them afloat until he could help them refinance the company.

His name was John Willys.

But, meanwhile, Chapin and Coffin had plans up their sleeves for an organization of their own. With a company under their own management they would have free scope for both production and design. Coffin was a clever engineer and brilliant in design; Chapin was a wonderfully good salesman and an able financier.

Having made up his mind that they would go into business together, Chapin resigned from his position with Olds and went to California for a vacation and to interest capital in this project. Those who had money to invest were more or less afraid of such a radical venture as the automobile business, yet he was making headway when he met E. R. Thomas of Buffalo, known as the builder of the " Thomas Flyer." They talked the proposition over at length and completed arrangements to start a plant in Detroit, building a car similar to the Olds.

Chapin was twenty-six when with Thomas, Howard E. Coffin, F. O. Bezner, and J. J. Brady, he organized the Thomas-Detroit Company. They started in a little match factory which belonged to Louis Mendelssohn. Later, Mendelssohn furnished the money to back the Fisher Body Company and became its first financial head.

The original investment in the Thomas-Detroit amounted to $150,000, all of which was put up in cash. Chapin and his associates raised half of their subscriptions personally, and the balance was furnished by local banks which loaned it to them on blue-prints and their reputation. From the first, Detroit banks supported and encouraged the automobile industry, and to their farsighted loans and wise counsel is due much of the success of the young financiers who asked their aid.

Among those who helped them was Alexander McPherson, president of the Old Detroit National, a canny old Scotsman who had a real ambition to see the boys succeed. He backed Chapin and the rest of his crowd from the very first, even as far back as 1906. Five years later Chapin became a director of the bank.

By this time Chapin had an acquaintance which was of the greatest value in the introduction of a new car. He knew the dealers all over the country. He had traveled extensively and understood requirements in different localities. The Olds had been the money maker among the cars, and the dealers of the country were keenly interested in what the new organization was going to turn out. By the time it began producing Thomas-Detroit cars the dealers were lined up and the output for the first year, 506 cars, was sold before it left the shipping department. To-day, the Hudson plant turns out more cars every day than this entire first-year output.

A keen analysis of markets showed them that there was a demand for a lower priced car. To build it they must produce in quantity. The Thomas-Detroit was selling at $2,750, and there were no low-priced four-cylinder motor vehicles.

At this time (1907) Chapin, Coffin, Bezner, and Brady owned one-third of the stock of the Thomas-Detroit Company. They persuaded Thomas to sell a block of stock to Hugh Chalmers, changed the name to Chalmers-Detroit, and brought out the four-cylinder Chalmers-Detroit 30 at $1,500. An immediate success was scored and great plant expansion was undertaken. They decided an even smaller car might be a money maker. A subsidiary company was formed and a college mate of Coffin, Roscoe B. Jackson, was put in charge of development. Previous to this he had been factory manager of the Olds Motor Works and he was then general manager of the Thomas Motor Company in Buffalo. To-day he is president of the Hudson company.

Jackson threw himself wholeheartedly into the plan, for the company was still in the process of formation when he took hold. J. L. Hudson, capitalist, well known in Detroit and a relative of Jackson, became interested and was asked to take the presidency of the company. For him the car was named.

In financing the Hudson barely enough money was put in for development — about $20,000. A canvass among dealers proved that the car had such possibilities that it was found easy to sell the output in advance, and the company was largely financed by this means. And ever since then expansion has been financed entirely out of earnings.

After the Hudson got its stride the Chapin and

Chalmers groups decided to separate their interests. This put Chapin, Bezner, and Coffin in Hudson control; J. L. Hudson became chairman of the board, and Chapin assumed the presidency.

One of the most important features of Hudson development has been the teamwork. Whenever a man showed special ability the company made stock arrangements with him. A certain amount of stock was set aside in his name and the dividends were credited against it until it was paid for. Under this plan most of the executives have fortunes of their own and stability of management has been secured.

Few men, either East or West, have attained in so few years the standing which has been accorded to Roy D. Chapin. As chairman of the board of the Hudson Motor Car Company, he devotes much of his time to public interests. From the very first he realized that the development of the rural sections of America was largely dependent on the condition of the highways, and he made a special study of road conditions in this country and abroad, attaining such a reputation as an authority that as soon as we entered the war he was called to Washington to head the Highways Transport Committee of the Council of National Defense. This committee was entrusted with the war-time energizing of highway transportation and began a development which has had a far-reaching effect on the entire problem of highway traffic. Since the war he has been connected with most of the broad movements which have had for their aim the making of our roads a medium for the quick and economical transport of men and goods.

In aeronautics, Mr. Chapin is not only an active enthusiast but has aided materially in its national development. He is probably one of the most expert private photographers in this country, and not only does wonderful portraits and beautiful landscapes, but is also an experienced operator with a moving picture camera. He is vice-president and a director in the National Automobile Chamber of Commerce, and is one of its most active workers. He was one of the organizers and is vice-president of the Lincoln Highway Association. As a member of the semi-governmental Highway Education Board, he is one of the leaders in educational work pertaining to highway engineering and highway transport.

But in all his successes and in spite of his large outside interests his loyalty to Detroit has been an outstanding factor, and he has always been identified with many of its prominent business enterprises. For years he has been a director in the First National Bank, which succeeded the Old Detroit National; he is vice-president of the Detroit Symphony Society, director of the Detroit Community Fund, and has taken an active part in all progressive local movements. From the first he has believed in Detroit, not merely as a great manufacturing center, but as a leader in civic enterprises.

Not only from the business but from the personal

side, life has been to him a well-rounded success. Ten years ago he married a charming Southern girl, who shares with him every interest of his busy life, and his residence at Grosse Pointe Farms is the center of a happy family life.

Roy Chapin is still so young that one stands aghast to remember all he has accomplished; but he had already arrived when most men of his years were still struggling in the ranks. Throughout his career he has always ranked as the youngest executive of his class in the automobile industry.

WALTER P. CHRYSLER

ONE sweltering forenoon in August, 1906, a man stood in the doorway of the shops of the Chicago Great Western Railroad. As he watched, the noon whistle blew and the men began to file out. In their anxiety to reach the open air they jostled against one another and crowded the forward line impatiently.

As they trickled out through the doorways the man followed them. He watched them moving off in groups, some of them aimlessly, others taking a more direct route. Many of them were men whose hair was streaked with grey — good mechanics, all of them. He thought of the rows of little brick houses where they lived, two families in a house. Nice, respectable little homes, clean as a pin, most of them; but was that all life had to offer?

At that time he was superintendent of motive power of the road. He had come up in nine years from those very shops. At thirty-three he was the youngest man who had ever held a position of that importance. He had won it through sheer driving power of will, an almost uncanny mechanical ability, and that marvelous capacity for turning out work which still makes him one of the wonders in the automotive industry.

As he crossed the yard he took a swift account of his abilities. He knew he had qualities which he had never used. One of them was a certain interest in finance. It irked him to see inefficient management, shortsighted policies, waste and ineffective effort. He had vision, but he was often handicapped in using it, for his work lay largely along the mechanical side; he gloried in responsibility, but he was at the top of his particular heap. Regardless of ability, he felt he had reached a place where promotion was impossible, for one of the inflexible laws of railroading is that a mechanical man never reaches the executive's chair.

Suddenly he came to a stop right in the middle of the yard. In that instant he sensed the difficulty. He was on the wrong side of the desk. Instead of repairing cars and running trains, he wanted to build and sell. It was not enough to do other people's bidding; he wanted to use his own judgment and foresight. It was the turning point in Walter P. Chrysler's career. From that moment he determined to blaze his own trail.

This story is important because it gives a swift picture of Chrysler's uncanny ability to get at the heart of things. When it came to him that he was on the wrong track for big advancement he did not hesitate to give up the position which had been the result of nine years of unremitting labor and start again in the shops of a new company where he could build under competitive conditions.

The American Locomotive Company's Pittsburgh works was in need of a works manager and Chrysler asked for the job, feeling that by utilizing his knowledge of the mechanical side and at the same time developing his genius for management and finance, he could not only hold the job but make it a stepping stone on the upward trail. He got it and went to work with a will. He soon found that he could use all his knowledge of shop practice and that in addition he would secure just what he had sought for, the opportunity to figure comparative and competitive costs. Within two years he had made such a study of non-productive effort, waste, and the value of increased individual output that the shop was being run at a big profit, and he was asked to become general manager of the company.

But all this time his mind had been racing far ahead of his actual accomplishment. While he was still superintendent of the Great Western Railroad he had become interested in the automobile. At first the appeal was purely mechanical, but later his clear vision saw in it a magnificent opportunity.

"As I visualized its future," Chrysler said in telling me about it, "it far outran railway development, which in a sense had reached its zenith, because the automobile provided flexible, economical, individual transportation which could be utilized for either business or pleasure. It knew no limits except a right-of-way, it was bounded by no greater restrictions than individual effort and will. To me it was the transportation of the future and as such I wanted to be a part of it. That was where I saw opportunity."

It so happened that about this time Charles W.

Nash had succeeded W. C. Durant as head of General Motors. It was the same Nash who had moved up from the Buick company, which he had been so successful in building up. Bankers are always on the lookout for live men to head the organizations for which they are assuming the financial responsibility, and the banking fraternity was following closely Chrysler's achievements at Pittsburgh.

The upshot of it was that he was called to head Buick production under Mr. Nash — and such was his genius for organization and accomplishment that the Buick product became one of the most talked-of cars in the automobile field. Into this constructive effort for his company Chrysler put all that was best of him, body and soul. Day and night he worked with a power possible only to a man of his remarkable vigor. He scoured the country for experts to add to his already notable staff. He worked with them through endless sessions to perfect even the smallest details that went into the make-up of the Buick car. He devised new tests for metals, enforced greater exactness in trying out the engines, changed the old wooden body to a neat steel body of simpler and more elegant design, and, incidentally, raised the production of Buick cars from about forty to close to 600 a day within a period of eight years, in addition to supervising and building an enormous new plant. When he left the company its net profits were in excess of $48,000,000 a year.

All this energy and interest had for its foundation

a simple incident of the days when he was still with the Great Western Railroad. Those were the early days of the automobile show, and the cars were still objects of curiosity, especially to expert mechanicians. This interest drew Chrysler and he went to the Chicago show with no other intention than to make a study of the mechanical side of the cars.

One of the outstanding features of the show was a huge white car upholstered with unusual elegance in bright red leather. From the moment he entered the show that particular car held Chrysler's attention. It held every one's, for that matter, for it came pretty near being the king pin about which the show revolved. He listened to the purr of its engines, he studied it forward, aft, and amidships. He went home at night and dreamed about it, and then came back to the show in the morning to examine it again.

Chrysler had saved up $700. He had a wife and two children. His salary was not large and his prospects were in no way remarkable. The price of the car was $5,000. He borrowed $4,300, and bought it. To talk of the incident still stirs him.

"When my wife heard about it it nearly broke up the family," he said, " for we were doing without many things in those days, but there was some urge within me which *made* me buy that car. When I got it home I promptly took it to pieces, and I think that in the three years it was in my possession I pulled it to pieces altogether about forty times."

From that time on Chrysler was obsessed with the

idea of building automobiles, and through all his construction work at the American Locomotive Company that thought was always dormant in the back of his mind. It was really the foundation of his entrance into the automobile field.

When Chrysler left General Motors in 1920, he was president of Buick and first vice-president of General Motors. In the few years of his connection with that company he had become one of the best-known production men in this country. He left them to take over the job of helping to put the Willys-Overland company back on its feet.

In the great shake-down which followed in the wake of the armistice, many of the companies had suffered, and the Willys-Overland was one of them. It was over manned, was carrying enormous inventories which it could not reduce, and its heavy commitments were burying the company under an investment which it could not swing. When Chrysler first came on the scene the company's bank loans totaled $46,000,000. Within a short time they had been reduced to $18,000,000. It was done by accepting the daily quotas until the makers of parts had absorbed their own high-priced material, and in the meantime he built up the distribution of Overland cars until the agents had been relieved of their overstock and were once more on their feet.

Right in the middle of this nerve-racking job came the call to the aid of the Maxwell-Chalmers company, at that time in serious difficulties. Its indebtedness to banks amounted to $18,000,000. It also owed creditors $14,000,000. It was said to be within twenty-four hours of bankruptcy, and conditions were so serious that settlement would have been at approximately 20 cents on the dollar. Information given Mr. Chrysler was that the company had 26,000 cars scattered all over the country, many of them still in transit. They were being held on sidings, in freight cars, and other places of storage. Notes receivable to the amount of $10,000,000 which required liquidation were being held against these cars. Worst of all, the company's product had been discredited, and he would have to face, not alone the company's indebtedness, but its reinstatement to a position of confidence in the public eye and in the automobile world.

It is indicative of Chrysler's disposition that all these difficulties only whetted his eagerness. Not only did he accept the proposition, but he got right to work. It meant two jobs instead of one, each of them bigger than the ordinary man would want to tackle, but that was the very thing which caught his interest.

One of the outstanding accomplishments of 1924 was the rapid success of the Chrysler Six, for the Chrysler Company during its first twelve months did a larger gross business than any other company during its first year. And at the same time the Maxwell company had one of the best years in its history.

The credit for this enormous advance should be placed where it belongs — on Chrysler's shoulders.

"What is the secret of your ability to make going

concerns out of these bankrupt companies?" I asked Mr. Chrysler.

"The first thing I do when I start to look into the affairs of a failing company is to study the personnel of the organization and the individuality of the men. I am concerned first of all with executives, because if their principles are not right it is useless to look for results from the men. When I have measured up in my own mind the capacity of the executives, I get out into the operation of the plant and watch the men. I look around to see how many of them are standing still and how many of them are moving around the plant. Highly paid workmen should be busy with accomplishment, not useless motion. If there is a lot of movement I know the plant is being badly operated.

"I do not believe in idle machines or idle men. Outside of the idle investment involved, it is bad policy. If a man is working next to an idle machine it not only has a bad effect on him mentally, but he takes less care of his own machine because he thinks he has a ready substitute. I believe in keeping people out of temptation, for many of them cannot resist it.

"I have the floor space measured and estimate the amount of its productive capacity and then check up to see whether it is overcrowded or is running under its capacity, also whether the plant is overmanned. If it is over manned and we are over-producing, I reduce the force arbitrarily." (Chrysler has often been criticized for his drastic reduction methods. He says that if expenses are too high they must be cut and cut *immediately*. There is no use letting them run on another minute.) " I proceed to get the organization into shape by cutting out every unnecessary expense and wasteful practice *the minute I discover it*. Some forms of non-productive effort are necessary in every organization, because all forms of service are not productive in themselves, even though they contribute to the general plan; but to allow wasteful practices to continue after they have been analyzed and proved wasteful is to sap the energy of your organization at its source."

At one time while Mr. Chrysler was with Buick, money was wanted for a larger sheet metal plant. Mr. Chrysler investigated and gave orders that the "trackers" should come to work at 8 instead of 7, that they should work during the noon hour when the plant was clear, and should also work an hour later than the rest of the force. During the noon hour and the last hour of the day the plant was cleared of finished products and raw materials put in their place. That meant that when the men came to work in the morning and after lunch they found raw materials awaiting them. The result of the order was that no new building was needed and the production of the plant was speeded up without the expenditure of a single cent. That is typical of the way in which Chrysler works. When all is explained it seems very simple.

"The majority of men pay too much attention to the way stations and not enough to the terminals," Chrysler said in speaking of meeting difficulties. "When railroad engineers come to a mountain they do not always go *through* it; sometimes it is best to go *around* it. Success comes through a judicious expenditure of energy. Sometimes it takes less to go around, and serves the same purpose. Men should look *forward*, and progress stops when they refuse to listen to other people's opinions, although they should make their own decisions. I never want to get to the place where I so dominate the job that no one under me dares to make suggestions."

It is interesting to note right here that every so often ten or fifteen of the biggest dealers in Chrysler's cars are called to the factory to offer new suggestions as to the output and distribution. And he listens to what they have to say, adopting all feasible measures.

Like all big and successful executives Chrysler has a wonderful ability to judge men.

"I gauge them through my intuition and experience," he replied in answer to my question as to how he did it. "Then, too, these cuts in the organization give me a big opportunity to learn something about my man power. I find out how much fight the men have in them and learn a lot about their individual force. By cutting to the quick I get rapid contacts and am able to measure up my men's resourcefulness under emergency conditions without delay."

Chrysler's great strength has always been his ability

to cut costs. When he goes into a new organization he first establishes the volume of business and then decides on the amount of the financial quota. He works entirely on a budget system. Every office and department is budgeted and is operated strictly on that basis. All sheets carry in detail from month to month a statement of all productive and non-productive labor in that department.

"We then have our statisticians set up the amount necessary for administrative purposes," said Mr. Chrysler, "which is based on a conservative quota. The items cover the capacity of the plant, productive labor, non-productive labor, productive materials, non-productive materials, all fixed charges, depreciations, sales administration, and executive administration. These are all counted in on the cost per car.

"Next we estimate our inventory turnover per year and our turnover of sight drafts from shipping the cars, so that we can see the rapidity of cash returns. They average about fifteen days. Cash requirements for credits and operating expenses are also carefully figured. Retail sales are followed closely, and production is increased or decreased in proportion to sales.

"We pay the strictest attention to each individual territory by counties, even analyzing our situation to the extent of determining what the dealer and we ourselves lose in profit on a territory when it fails to sell its quota. We estimate this both for ourselves and for the dealer, to see what each one of us has lost and, when necessary, we send out men to help the dealers check their records."

Confronted with the necessity of disposing of over-production in quick order, Chrysler has developed some remarkable distribution principles. Jumping from operating to sales, he is quick to measure them and see whether they are equal to plant capacity, but he goes on record as unalterably opposed to loading up his dealers in order to move over-production.

"To force on your dealers more cars than they can sell is not only poor business, but also not constructive selling," he says. "Our agents all carry less than thirty days' stock, except where shipments might be delayed in reaching them, as for example on the Pacific Coast. We do not feel that it is fair to our dealers to let them tie up their money in large stocks, but we do expect them to merchandise up to our quota standards. We look after them closely and try to help them make the quick turnover we feel to be one of the big points of our business.

"All territories are operated on a quota basis, the quotas being set at the home office. We base the establishment of the quota on the actual volume of automobile sales of all makes in the past in that territory, and then figure our percentage to the total sales. Quotas are often unfair, for they are not set on actual conditions. Past sales are a reality and you are not unfair to a man when you ask him to sell a share of what is being sold. We feel this system is just, because if general business in a given territory falls off we are not expecting unreasonable things of our representatives. Often an injustice is very apparent to the men, whereas the organization is perfectly ignorant that it is expecting any more of them than it should. Where sales fall off in a given territory we send our sales expert there immediately and he gives the dealer the benefit of his expert advice."

I have told you of Chrysler, the executive, but his human side is no less interesting. He is a driving power, a beautifully balanced, smoothly running engine, but his dynamic energy is not restricted to his business, and as he has risen in power he has never lost the human touch.

Once, at an important conference in San Francisco, when time was precious as gold, there came a clamor at the door and out of it a brogue so thick you could have cut it with a knife. It was an old chum of Chrysler's who had worked side by side with him on an engine in the early days. Did Chrysler go out to see him? He did. And he made an appointment to have lunch with him the next day.

Mr. Chrysler early in 1926 financed an expedition to the African jungle for the purpose of bagging a hundred or more live specimens of rare wild animals for the National Zoo at Washington.

Chrysler's personal story is one of absorbing interest. He started as a wiper of locomotives, at five cents an hour; within sixteen years he was building them. At seventeen he entered the Union Pacific shops as a machinist's apprentice and lived on what he made, which was 7½ cents an hour. Whenever somebody wanted a man willing to do a hot, dirty job, they called Chrysler; he never side-stepped, and he always made good.

O. D. F.

W. C. DURANT

WILLIAM C. Durant is, next to Henry Ford, the most spectacular figure in the automobile industry. They have little else, however, in common.

Ford, until recent years, concentrated all his attention on building up his business. His "Peace Ship" exploit was followed by his sensational and sustained attack upon the Jews. More recently, he has taken to the more innocent hobby of "collecting" inns and other places of historic interest and also old stagecoaches, sap buckets and various other antiques.

Durant, on the other hand, has repeatedly been mentioned conspicuously in Wall Street speculation. Whereas Wall Street has always been anathema to Ford, it has been a siren to Durant, luring him, according to all accounts, into tremendous speculative exploits, sometimes extremely profitable, sometimes contributing to his undoing.

Those who know Durant best declare that both times he lost his power the cause was partly his speculative proclivities.

But they also claim that, had he left Wall Street alone, he probably would have become — and remained — a dominating figure in the automobile industry, for, they declare emphatically, he has the most brilliant of brains, inexhaustible energy, tremendous ambition, a profound insight into human nature, and courage unlimited. His friends also know him as one of the "best-hearted" fellows who ever walked in shoe leather or rode in an automobile, and they tell you that no other leader has as many friends in the industry and outside the industry.

I personally know of many incidents illustrating Durant's unselfishness and generosity. He has done for others far more than many men whose names are blazoned in the newspapers as wonderful philanthropists.

I am convinced that Durant's chief ambition never has been to roll up scores and scores of millions of dollars for himself. His is not a mercenary ambition. He loves power; he constantly itches to accomplish big things. Even his stock market exploits have not been conducted for the sole purpose of enriching his own pocket, but often have been inspired by the idea of benefiting those interested in his companies and of swelling his power to do bigger things in his own field.

The results, however, have proved the truth of the decree, "No man can serve two masters," and of the axiom that no man can reach and remain at the summits of business success if he keeps only one eye on his business and the other on the stock ticker.

When Durant fell from his high place in the automobile world the second time, in 1920, some of his closest friends gave emphatic assurances that he had been effectively and finally cured of his weakness for stock market speculation and that he would devote his entire time and attention to regaining a shining place in the automobile industry.

Unfortunately, these assurances have not been borne out by the facts as reported almost daily from Wall Street after the sensational boom in stocks set in when President Coolidge was elected. No other one name, not even that of Jesse L. Livermore, was so frequently and prominently mentioned in connection with the phenomenal sky-rocketing in certain industrial stocks. Wall Street scribes found fascinating interest in computing the number of millions Durant rolled up in this, that and the next stock which doubled or trebled in quoted value between November and March.

What will the end be? Will Durant, after his previous bitter experiences, have sense enough this time to cash in his Wall Street paper profits and turn his undivided attention to retrieving his place at the very front of automobile producers? Or, will his Wall Street activities reduce his importance as an automobile producer?

It was because I had grave doubts concerning the policies being pursued by William C. Durant after he launched his Durant Motors, Inc., Star Motors, and half-a-hundred affiliated projects that I, as a financial writer, felt it a duty to the public to question the wisdom of investors and others in clamoring to buy Durant Motors shares, originally issued to insiders for $10, at what seemed to be the unwarrantedly high quotations of $70 to $84. My questions and criticisms brought upon my head a deluge of denunciatory letters from the myriads of Durant's friends and followers. Some of them accused me of being bribed by Morgan interests or by the duPonts or by "Wall Street." Some demanded to know "What has Durant ever done to you?"

Durant did to me just as much as all these alleged bribes amounted to — nothing. I was sincerely anxious to induce the public to do some sober thinking, for the public showed pronounced symptoms of having been carried away by his plans and promises. I was also anxious — although I won't be believed — to do what I could to keep Durant on the right track.

I am willing to be judged by the events that followed. At the time I attempted to present the cold facts and to raise doubts as to the wisdom of climbing for the Durant stocks, Durant Motors shares were selling around $70 and had been selling above $80. An army of 2,000 salesmen were out ringing door bells, and so successful were their efforts to enroll buyers of Durant stocks on the installment plan that more than a quarter-of-a-million stockholders were quickly booked, and Durant had visions of attracting more than half-a-million.

When I asked him whether he did not have qualms about gathering in and becoming responsible for the life savings of so many families, he explained that his theory was to induce thousands of families who had never saved a dollar to start paying for these securities bit by bit out of weekly earnings. He described this movement as one of the most important thrift campaigns ever undertaken. The terms on which the shares were sold prohibited the buyers from disposing of them until a date quite some distance in the future, Durant's contention being that this would prevent holders from being induced to part with their shares before their worth could be properly demonstrated by the payment of generous dividends.

Without questioning Durant's motives, I could not but feel that his optimism had outrun conservatism and that the rosy results pictured were unlikely to materialize in the measurably near future. I could not but form this conclusion notwithstanding that — as many letter-writers pointed out to me — Durant had earned an almost unique reputation for having "made money for his followers."

The records show that the Durant Motors stocks never again rose above $80 but moved down and down until finally they went as low as $10 in 1925, proving that my questioning of the soundness of the phenomenal boosting of the shares was timely and abundantly warranted.

In March, 1926, $6 was touched. Whereas I felt it a public duty to urge caution when the shares were selling at three or four times that figure, I have no word of advice to offer one way or the other regarding the purchasing of shares around their lower level. Durant may again brilliantly demonstrate his ability to "come back." Or, he may not. I, for one, sincerely hope, for the sake of the several hundred thousand families who have invested their savings in his securities, as well as for his own sake, that he will be able to raise his enterprises to a stable, solid, dividend-paying basis.

Without question, William C. Durant's career has been marked by extraordinary talents. In one favorable account of his achievements, published in " Motor " for January, 1923, the writer, W. A. P. Johns, says:

" There is ample reason for the public at large to consider W. C. Durant as a spectacular Wall Street operator — instead of a man whose inexhaustible energy has brought huge and successful industrial enterprises into being; ample reason to believe him a financial operator whose pyrotechnic dexterity amazed the banking world — instead of an able manufacturer who almost twenty years ago sensed the future of the automobile and built against that future; ample reason to look on him as the master plunger — instead of the master builder; ample reason to look on him as a man who worships money — instead of one who worships at the shrine of achievement; ample reason for all this, and why?

" Simply because until two years ago W. C. Durant rarely talked for publication, preferring the undisturbed quiet of the pilot house.

" I propose to disillusion you, and to enable you a few years hence to nod your head in a knowing way when understanding men assert, 'He is one of the great constructive geniuses of the automotive industry.' "

As a young man William Crapo Durant was a rolling stone, a jack of many trades — but it wouldn't be correct to say that he was master of none. He showed many-sided ability. Although he was born in Boston (in 1861) the family moved to Flint, Michigan, then little more than a village. His first job was in a humble grocery store operated in connection with his grandfather's mill. Next he worked in the mill as a common laborer before being promoted to a machine and later to the position of inspector. Meanwhile, he acted as clerk at night in a drug store. Among its wares was a patent medicine. Durant thought he saw possibilities in it, and he accordingly gave up his job to travel the surrounding country selling this cure-all to farmers.

Next he became a clerk in a cigar store, and then traveling salesman. Here he corralled so many orders that the other three salesmen were let go. From selling cigars to selling insurance was his next step. From insurance he turned to real estate. Next he became secretary of Flint's privately-owned, down-at-the-heels water works, at $25 a month. He spent much of his time interviewing dissatisfied customers, and then he rapidly and successfully eliminated the causes for dissatisfaction.

Happening to get a lift one day in a two-wheel road cart, he noted its attractive construction, learned that it was built at Coldwater, Michigan, boarded a train for that city, and within twenty-four hours had contracted to purchase the entire business for $2,000 —

which he didn't possess. A chum, J. Dallas Dort, a clerk in a hardware store, agreed to put up $1,000 to become half-owner of what was named the Durant-Dort Carriage Company. Even after all these varied experiences, Durant had reached only his twenty-fifth birthday.

It is perhaps significant, in the light of subsequent events, that Durant took charge of *finance* and sales and that Dort became responsible for production. Here Durant demonstrated his ability to do big things. The late J. P. Morgan once told Judge Gary that he regarded the formation of the Federal Steel Company, by Judge Gary, as a greater achievement than the formation, later, of the United States Steel Corporation. What Durant did in the horse-drawn vehicle field really deserves to be ranked with the biggest of his achievements in the motor field. Very rapidly — Durant is a rapid operator — the tiny business was developed into the largest in America, with fourteen plants here and in Canada producing 150,000 vehicles a year.

It perhaps affords another clue to the make-up of Durant to know that at this early stage of his career he had a bad failure; an ambitious bicycle venture, in which he sold stock to outsiders, came a cropper.

Not satisfied with his colossal carriage-building business nor profiting by his bitter experience with that side-line, Durant took on another, an accessory company. It also proved a fizzle.

But let it be recorded, for this also is characteristic

of Billy Durant, that he made good the losses suffered by those who invested in these two unfortunate projects. Durant even then was no mercenary money-grabber, bent only upon enriching himself regardless of the cost or consequences to others. Not every young man eager to make a splash in the world has such scruples. This phase is just as noteworthy a characteristic of the real Durant as the other outstanding phase, his rapid-fire successes and his setbacks.

Brilliant success crowned Durant's next important — and destined to become epochal — move. Invited to take hold of the tottering Flint Wagon Works, which had boldly ventured to produce a horseless vehicle, later known as the Buick automobile, Durant found the local citizens ready to supply half-a-million dollars of cash to save this, the oldest and largest factory in the city. For undertaking this task Durant received $202,000 common stock which, to his credit be it said, he transferred to the Durant-Dort Carriage Company.

Thus did William C. Durant invade the infant automobile industry. The year was 1903.

His ambition was to become the greatest builder of automobiles, just as he had previously become the greatest builder of horse-drawn vehicles. Quick worker though he was, it took him some time to get going. The 1903 production of Buick was 16, the 1904 production 28. Then Durant got steam up. The next year he built and sold 627, and in the panic year of 1907 no fewer than 2,295.

W. C. DURANT

Such was his faith that he put more than 2,000 men to work on vast expansions to his plants. More; he reached out and acquired control of the fledgling Cadillac Company, the struggling Oldsmobile, and the floundering Oakland, and gathered them into a $10,000,000 organizaton, the General Motors Corporation, late in 1908.

Net profits the next year exceeded the total capitalization and in the following year were still larger. "Bigger! Bigger!! Bigger!!!" Some fairy — or evil spirit — apparently kept whispering and still keeps whispering this incitement into Durant's ear. He kept expanding in this, that and other directions.

Durant's scant regard for money has oftener than once contributed to his undoing. Then, as later, he underrated the vital part it plays in business. His ambitions widened and widened like the waves in the wake of a vast, giant liner. He borrowed and borrowed without making certain that he could meet all the obligations thus incurred.

Then came the first sensational Durant tumble from power. He needed at least $15,000,000 to avert bankruptcy. The financial powers refused to entrust this sum to the man who had been responsible for the over-expansion. To save the situation, Durant agreed to step down and let the capitalistic interests control the company through a voting trust of the common stock for five years.

But Durant did not let grass grow under his feet. Backed by several associates, he organized the Chevrolet Motor Company in his home city, Flint. Producing a low-priced car, Durant gradually worked up a large output. In a very few years his company was earning generous profits.

Meanwhile, September, 1915, the expiration of the General Motors voting trust, was approaching. Whereas General Motors shares had sunk as low as $24, they began to rise, at first moderately, then spectacularly. They doubled, trebled, quadrupled in price until they touched a figure eleven times the minimum quotation.

The General Motors meeting on September 15, 1915, furnished Wall Street one of the most sensational and surprising incidents in its history. W. C. Durant astounded Wall Street and every one else by disclosing that he held enough stock to control the meeting!

He immediately caused the $15,000,000 to be paid off and he also declared a cash dividend of $50 a share. Durant was back in the saddle, whip in hand and wearing spurs. Chevrolet, through which Durant had operated to regain control, became a unit of General Motors. He also formed United Motors, an accessory holding company.

Now followed another period of Napoleonic expansion. Instead of having learned caution, Durant launched on a more ambitious series of adventures than ever before. His actions flouted the well-proved adage, " No tree ever quite reaches heaven." His aspirations knew no limits.

How fast and furiously Durant steamed ahead in

W. C. DURANT

the next few years can be deduced from this statement by his friendly biographer:

"I saw a letter dated January 21, 1920, from an important member of the finance committee, commenting upon the company's growth through the year 1919. Two sentences are worthy of exact transcription 'In other words, General Motors to-day is eight times as large as the company the bankers were managing. This is a fine tribute to your foresight.'"

Alas, events were to demonstrate that what was being then — and later — so feverishly exercised was not fine foresight, but lack of foresight. Let us again quote from Durant's staunch biographical champion:

"Earning at the rate of twelve-and-one-half to thirteen millions of dollars a month, General Motors went into a scheme of expansion the like of which has never been attempted in the automobile or any other industry. The corporation's capital was voted up to more than one billion dollars. Fifty million shares of no par value stock were authorized. Stock dividends were voted that would release five hundred thousand shares of common each quarter.

"A housing and dormitory program involving over $33,000,000 was set under way. An office building to cost over $20,000,000 was begun in Detroit. Various factories were radically expanded. New and very costly plants were constructed at peak prices. United Motors Corporation was absorbed and other divisions were acquired for cash or by stock exchange.

"All this called for untold millions — for so many,

many millions that the corporation, instead of having a cash surplus of $106,000,000 in the banks as at the first of the year, owed its banks $80,000,000 and was obligated in other ways for an additional $120,000,000. In other words, the execution of the expansion plan had required over $300,000,000 — had drastically reduced the liquid working capital and had tied up a vast sum in fixed investment.

"I saw a most comprehensive chart prepared, not by Mr. Durant, but by his associates, covering a period of eight future years, and setting forth the results of the plan, year by year. And the last year, according to the estimate, would see the company using over $1,000,000,000 liquid capital, earning 142 per cent. on its outstanding common stock, which would have a market value of $1,000 a share!"

The public naturally assumed, since W. C. Durant was head of General Motors, that he was responsible for this expansion program. Durant never publicly repudiated it. His previous gigantic activities made the public ready to accept this latest exploit as characteristic of Durant. His biographer claims, however, that Durant was not responsible for, but antagonistic to the program. He says he knows who was responsible but won't tell.

However that may be, the fact is that once again Durant found himself fatally over-expanded. Wall Street took fright. General Motors shares began to collapse, as did many other shares following the bursting of the post-war boom. Down — down — down —

went General Motors stock. Starting around $40, it was approaching $30 when Durant organized a buying syndicate, to whom, it is said, he gave personal guarantee against loss. The debacle continued. He formed another buying syndicate. The headlong tumbling was not arrested. One day towards the end of July (1920) heavy selling orders carried the stock to the edge of $20. Durant boldly but vainly kept on buying. But still demoralization grew worse and worse. The shares broke to $18, to $16, to $14, to $12.

Then he gave up. He owed millions upon millions to financial and brokerage concerns and was unable to meet demands for payment. An S. O. S. went out.

Bluntly, Durant's obligations were taken over and so was everything he possessed, except his beautiful home at Deal, N. J., and, it was understood, a considerable block of General Motors stock held in the name of Mrs. Durant.

J. P. Morgan & Company, in association with the duPont interests, headed by Pierre duPont (who had earlier become financially interested), did the salvaging and consequently took over control.

On December 1, 1920, Durant, it is related, visited his office for the last time as president of General Motors and walked out with the remark to associates, "Well, May first is usually national moving day, but we seem to be moving on December first."

You probably have been at same gathering where some one has shouted, "Are we downhearted?" and back has come a deafening roar, "No-o-o-o!" Did

Durant do what many men would have done at his age, almost sixty? No. Instead of stepping down and out and remaining down and out, the very next month he organized and incorporated Durant Motors " without a car, without a plant, without a hammer, without a single piece of steel — without anything but W. C. Durant and the faith of his friends."

A few months later the Durant Four made its appearance, and in less than a year after organization the Star made a debut which attracted extraordinary interest. It was going to compete with the Ford. Other products were announced with amazing rapidity, including the Flint, the Princeton, the Eagle, the Durant Special, the Mason Truck, the Locomobile. An army of more than 2,000 stock salesmen was sent out to sell Durant Motors and Star Company shares on the installment plan to individuals and families of small means, and in quick order a quarter-of-a-million subscribers were enrolled. Colossal schemes were launched. Plans for a national bank to be conducted on novel lines were published and the Liberty National Bank was promptly set going.

The name Durant was on everybody's tongue, in the industry and on the street. Durant Motors stock soared to $84 a share. The public's imagination was aflame.

The excitement, however, did not long remain at fever-heat. Some of the products didn't fulfil the intoxicating expectations which had been formed. Quotations for the Durant stocks began to subside.

Durant's name next broke into newspaper front pages by his activities in the shares of Fisher Body, of which, it became understood, he had acquired quite a block. Later his name began to be coupled with a precipitous rise in U. S. Cast Iron Pipe shares. When the stock market began to boil after Coolidge's election, Durant's name figured more prominently and frequently than that of any other speculator in the gossip of Wall Street. If stock market commentators could not find any reason for a particularly sensational rise in a stock, they dragged in the name of Durant.

After a rather long lull, Durant's Star car again began to attract public attention, Durant having put the marketing of it into the hands of Colin Campbell, an unusually dynamic hustler. The Flint car has won many converts. And one of the surprises at the 1925 Automobile Show in New York was the exhibition of a light, low-priced Locomobile, named the Junior Eight.

What of the future?

Unquestionably, Durant has abilities in certain directions not surpassed, perhaps not equalled, by any other man in the automobile industry. He has repeatedly demonstrated capacity for developing enterprises of staggering magnitude. But speculation and over-expansion have oftener than once proved his undoing.

What the end will be of the latest chapter Durant has been writing in very large and bold letters, the future alone can tell. After sustaining injury in a railway accident in January, 1926, he figured spectacularly in Wall Street reports of heroic attempts to check demoralization in the stock market, and this was followed by intimations that he had slackened his hold on the reigns of his automobile ventures.

We shall see what we shall see.

B. C. F.

ALBERT R. ERSKINE

"AMERICA has no traditions," Europeans often declare in superior tone.

Hasn't it?

What of Tiffany in jewelry? What of Marshall Field & Company in dry goods? What of the House of Morgan in international banking? What of Underwood and Remington in the field of typewriting? What of the Wright brothers, pioneer flyers? What of the name Singer in the sewing machine world? What of McCormick and Deering in the realm of agricultural machinery? What of Armour and Swift in the industry they created, packing? What of Patterson of cash register history? What of Edison? What of Alexander Graham Bell? What of the empire nurtured by James J. Hill, the greatest of all America's railroad builders. What of Pullman, father of railway sleeping cars? What of Goodyear, originator of the rubber industry? What of Robert Fulton, the first to ply a steamboat? What of Morse, who first joined together the Old World and the New by his strand of cable?

Suggest to A. R. Erskine that there are no traditions in America!

"Has Studebaker no traditions?" he will challenge you. "The name Studebaker has stood for all that is sound and honest and staunch and durable in vehicular transportation for more than seventy years. No business in America, no business in the whole world, has better traditions to live up to than we of the Studebaker Corporation have. Studebaker tradition, Studebaker reputation enters into the building of every car we produce."

True, America may be weak in historic traditions, weak in artistic and literary traditions, weak in architectural and social and poetic traditions. But when you turn to business, to industry, to invention, America has traditions and achievements not eclipsed by any country.

No other automobile company has roots stretching quite so far back as those of the Studebaker Corporation.

Ninety years ago and more Studebaker "covered wagons" were being built in Ohio for the pioneers then penetrating the Middle West — one of these "prairie schooners," built by John Studebaker in 1830, is to-day in the Studebaker museum at South Bend, Indiana.

In 1852, H. & C. Studebaker, sons of John Studebaker, opened a blacksmith and wagon-making shop at South Bend. Their capital was sixty-eight dollars, and their output the first year was two wagons. In 1925 Studebaker marketed 134,664 automobiles, and net sales amounted to $161,362,945 at wholesale prices. Net profits were $16,619,523, and dividends totalled $10,423,087. Employees averaged 21,977.

H. & C. Studebaker had two forges. To-day, 12,500 machines are used in 342 manufacturing departments. Over 1,200 inspectors are employed in the plants, and 96,000 inspection operations are provided for during the course of manufacture; 1,769 manufacturing operations are accurate to one-thousandth of an inch, and 564 to one-half-thousandth of an inch.

Thirty thousand tons of pig-iron, 130,000 tons of steel, 450,000 gallons of lacquers and enamels, 150,000 hides of leather, 1,778,000 square feet of plate glass, 20,745,000 board feet of lumber, 7,500,000 gallons of fuel oil, 160,000 tons of coal, and 275,000,000 cubic feet of gas are used annually.

Over 550,000 tests were made in 1923 of devices, machines, materials, and manufacturing operations by the research and experimental laboratories, engineering and methods and standards departments.

Five mammoth plants at South Bend, Detroit, and Walkerville (Ont.), covering 225 acres and containing 7,500,000 square feet of floor space, with 25 branch offices, 5,000 dealers, and 3,500 service stations, indicate the development from the original tiny shop.

Although Studebaker made history by becoming and remaining the largest manufacturer of horse-drawn vehicles for two generations, the greatest Studebaker history has been made since the war. In seven years $52,000,000 was expended for development of plant facilities, which made Studebaker the second-largest in plant facilities of the individual automobile manufacturers of the world.

One man has been mainly responsible for this phenomenal growth and prosperity, namely, Albert Russel Erskine.

Ford started as a mechanic; Sloan started as an engineer; Durant and Willys started as salesmen. Erskine was an expert accountant when he entered the automobile arena.

But he had a hard, industrious climb before he reached that point.

Born in Huntsville, Alabama, on January 24, 1871, of a long line of fine stock, including a great-grandfather who was a first lieutenant in the first Virginia regiment in the Revolutionary Army, young Russel early learned that the family fortune had been totally swept away by the Civil War, leaving in his home nothing but a cabinetful of Confederate bonds and money with which he used to "play store." His father, who had enlisted in the Confederate Army when only a boy of sixteen, moved first to Texas and then to St. Louis, where the young son attended public school.

When he was fifteen, the family moved back to Huntsville, but Russel went to work as office boy with the Mobile & Ohio Railroad. From $30 a month on this job he changed in two years to another where he soon got $10 a week through having learned how to keep the books by always offering to assist the regular bookkeeper. "I realized even then," Mr. Erskine recalls, "that the only way to get on was to learn to do better work."

ALBERT R. ERSKINE

His next step up was as bookkeeper with another concern in St. Louis, at $75 a month. Then, when another bookkeeper left, young Erskine went to the head of the firm with this suggestion: "I'll do both jobs if you will pay me $100 a month. I'll make $25 and you'll save $50 a month." His employer remarked, "I believe you can do it."

And Erskine did, even though it meant that for three years he never was absent a day through sickness or taking any vacation, notwithstanding that he worked late into the night very, very often.

When twenty-seven, Mr. Erskine was offered the position of chief clerk with the American Cotton Company, at St. Louis. But it was not long before he was drawn into headquarters at New York and made general auditor. Later he was given supervision of 320 cotton gins located all over the South. Here he devised a complete system of forms, reports, statements, etc., which presented a clear picture of the company's operations at all points. When, through poor management, the company was placed in receivership, young Erskine was the only official retained by the receivers.

Not relishing the idea of remaining with a dead company, he looked around for a connection with a live one. Hearing that the fine, old Yale & Towne Company was looking for a treasurer, Mr. Erskine said to himself, "I'm going to get that job." Mr. Towne was quite reserved at the first interview, but Mr. Erskine was confident that a perusal of the accounting and business code which he had compiled for the American Cotton Company would move Mr. Towne. It did.

"Come as an auditor and start at $100 a week," said Mr. Towne. "Audit our books and accounts for 1904 and if you suit us, you will be made our treasurer."

From eight to six every day Accountant Erskine kept his eyes glued to his work and attracted but little attention. Finally, Mr. Towne asked him to lunch, and then Mr. Erskine told him very plainly that his methods were expensive, overlapping, and not comprehensive. He outlined improvements. He was made treasurer before he completed the audit and later a director and member of the executive committee. Many of the methods Mr. Erskine then introduced are still in force.

To the vice-presidency of the Underwood Typewriter Company was Mr. Erskine's next step, in 1910. A banker friend who had followed Mr. Erskine's career informed him that the Studebaker Corporation was looking for new blood, an executive having knowledge of finance, accounting, etc. "It's worth $20,000 a year at the start," remarked the banker.

What was the first thing Mr. Erskine did when he joined the Studebaker Corporation, in October, 1911?

"I took no office, not even a desk," Mr. Erskine narrated to me. "I spent the first four months out in different departments. I went to the desks of the men in every department and asked them to show me what they were doing, how they were doing it and why they were doing it. I thus investigated the methods employed all through the plant.

"Having learned the details of the financial and commercial ends of the business, and having already had experience in modernizing corporation methods, I set about installing simple, direct and economical systems in these departments. I knew clerical operations that could be dispensed with, and also what employees should be removed.

"The departments were not organized on functional lines. For example, a great deal of accounting was done in the sales department and was duplicated in the accounting department. Now, sales departments exist to sell goods. Salesmen are not accountants. I divorced them from accounting entirely and scrapped most of the accounting and recording work they had been doing. The manufacturing department, the purchasing department, and other departments were similarly relieved of all record-keeping properly belonging to the accounting department.

"At South Bend and vehicle branch houses I found 3,500 forms in use. I cut them down to about 1,500. New forms were substituted for old ones as old ones were used up and within six months every department was functioning smoothly on the new systems, without knowing that it had taken any medicine.

"Next, all branch accounting was brought into headquarters. The function of a branch house is to sell automobiles, not to keep accounts. No branch manager should have to do office work. This not only saved money, but greatly improved the running of things."

The directors recognized Mr. Erskine's worth by electing him first vice-president in December, 1913, and he has been running the company ever since, although his formal election to the presidency did not come until eighteen months later, in July, 1915.

The Studebaker Corporation, as the company was named when organized in 1911, had only $9,800,000 in plant and property account and a capacity of only 22,000 cars a year, in addition to facilities for making 150,000 wagons and buggies a year.

The war broke out in Europe before Mr. Erskine had opportunity to get the automobile business going on a large scale, and so sure did he become that the United States would be drawn into the fray that, two months before Congress actually declared war, Studebaker's president sent this telegram to President Wilson:

"Studebaker factories, of course, are at the disposal of the Government. Any orders given us will receive preference and clear right-of-way."

President Wilson sent cordial thanks for what was probably the first offer received from any corporation to turn its plants over to the Government, and the War Department immediately opened negotiations with the corporation for the furnishing of large quantities of transport wagons, harness, ambulances, water carts, etc. At the drop of the war hat, the Studebaker plant swung into war work on such a scale that, within a month after hostilities started, automobile production was cut 50 per cent. Within a year there was another 50 per cent. cut, and before the war ended Studebaker was working 100 per cent. on Government orders.

Nothing in Mr. Erskine's whole career has yielded him more satisfaction than Studebaker's war record.

Meanwhile, just as Studebaker had been forehanded in preparing for war, it had been foresightedly preparing for peace. At the very start of the war, Mr. Erskine instructed his engineering department to apply themselves to designing an entirely new line of Studebaker automobiles and to ignore the old models.

On September 15, 1917, three cars were secretly rolled on a boat at Detroit and as secretly rolled off at Buffalo, where Mr. Erskine joined the engineers for the test. These cars were then driven through Canada and the United States, covering 20,000 miles. In December, they were put on the Chicago speedway and run constantly, night and day, for another 30,000 miles. Through snow storms and sleet storms and rain storms, through zero weather and thaws, one of the cars regularly covered 800 miles a day and the other (lighter) two, 600 miles. The most elaborate records were kept covering gas consumption, oil consumption, speed, repairs, etc., etc.

"These are the cars which made Studebaker famous," to quote Mr. Erskine. Since that time improvement and development have been constantly sought and the present series of models show the results. Many new features were incorporated in these cars, notable among them being the duplex top by which all of the disadvantages of the old-type top and curtains have been overcome and the so-called open car can be quickly converted into what practically amounts to a closed car. These models, announced in September, 1924, met with instant public approval and the demand has grown to such proportion that the plants became taxed to the utmost to fill the orders.

Studebaker has not only been made famous by its Big Six, its Special Six and its Standard Six, but it has also been made rich.

In 1921 the automobile industry, outside of Ford and Studebaker, did only 55 per cent. of the volume done in 1920, whereas Studebaker's record was 129 per cent. Sales later were: 1920, 51,474 cars; 1921, 66,643; 1922, 110,269; 1923, 145,167; 1924, 110,240; 1925, 134,664.

But these figures do not convey an adequate idea of the progress made. Remarkable though the expansion in output and profit has been, the most remarkable feat of all has been the strengthening of the corporation's plants by the addition of enlarged as well as new facilities to fit it to produce better cars at less cost and to be more independent of outside supplies. And all out of the company's own earnings.

Out of $131,000,000 of profits, of which $121,000,-000 have been made since Mr. Erskine became president, $52,000,000 have been put back into plants, bringing their total worth to $58,800,000, while $60,000,000 in cash and $30,000,000 in stock dividends have been paid to stockholders, and the balance added to surplus.

A $3,500,000 iron foundry, one of the largest and most modern in the world, has been built, capable of taking care of 1,000 cars a day. The company can now make all its own castings, thus saving one-half cent a pound, or $3,000 per day on castings alone. No less than $8,000,000 has been spent on closed body plants, dry kilns, etc., so that, to use Mr. Erskine's words, " No other individual manufacturer, except Ford, can produce as many closed bodies as we can and no manufacturer can make them better, because we have experienced wood workers and trimming craftsmen who used to make Studebaker carriages. In fact, with these new plants we can produce closed bodies at South Bend 10 per cent. cheaper than they can be made in Detroit. Therefore, we can sell closed cars cheaper than anybody in the industry.

" In 1922 we put up a building 767 feet long, 172 feet wide, and 4 stories high, of reinforced concrete, to enable us to manufacture 150 Standard Six closed bodies per day. In 1923 we erected a building 820 by 100 feet, 6 stories high, costing, with equipment, $2,500,000, and having a capacity of 150 Special Six and Big Six closed bodies per day. Additional equipment and improved methods installed and worked out in 1924 have raised the capacities of these buildings to

270 Standard Six closed bodies and 190 Special and Big Six closed bodies per day. In future we will make all our own bodies.

"We are able to do this because we were lucky," — Mr. Erskine's eyes twinkled as he used the word "lucky" — "in liquidating our horse vehicle business in 1919–20, through the regular trade channels, at full wholesale prices, for you will remember that everything was booming at that time and people couldn't get enough of anything. This gave us more room, more money and more men of unusual skill for the production of motor cars, particularly closed bodies. Had we not sold out then, we would doubtless have had to close down that whole part of our works in 1921."

Every automobile manufacturer believes, of course, that he turns out a superior car. The facts, however, talk. In a 1922 Studebaker advertisement this statement is made:

"Proof that the cars stand up in service with minimum repairs is evidenced by the fact that our sales of repair parts in 1921 were 12 per cent. less than they were in 1919, notwithstanding that 118,000 new cars were sold and put in operation in 1920 and 1921. Based on the total estimated number of Studebaker cars in operation in 1921, we sold $16 worth of parts per car for repairs from all causes, including accidents."

Since that advertisement was written proof of the increasing durability of Studebaker cars is found in the fact that for 1924 the sales of repair parts per car had fallen still further to $10.84.

ALBERT R. ERSKINE

There is only one subject on which Mr. Erskine talks more enthusiastically than he talks about Studebaker cars. This is Studebaker's workers.

I have never met an employer more interested in his work people or more elated over the generous treatment it has been possible to extend. Mr. Erskine likes to talk on this theme by the hour. It is possible here to give only a very brief summary of his statements:

"When I was made president in 1915 I took the position that the relations between labor and capital and management should be these:

"The first duty of an employer is to labor. By labor I mean any man that does what he is told. It is the duty of capital and management to compensate liberally, paying at least the current wage and probably a little more, and to give workers decent and healthful surroundings and treat them with the utmost consideration. If management cannot do this, then something is wrong.

"The next duty is to capital. Management should return to capital a liberal reward on the investment, say, 10 per cent. in our industry.

"If there are profits above this, I think management should receive a part of them.

"In 1915 we put into effect a bonus plan, benefiting some 400 men and women, from foremen up — every person having authority to manage employees or property, the tellers. This bonus was at first 20 per cent. after deductions for the return on the capital employed, but later, so large were profits, that the rate was cut to 10 per cent. If necessary, however, I would make it 50 per cent., for I believe that capital should be willing to go fifty-fifty with management after it has been well taken care of.

"In March, 1917, we inaugurated dividends on wages. Like other companies, we had had a very heavy labor turnover. There have always been millions of migratory workers, men who will not settle long enough anywhere to accomplish really effective work. We sought to provide a strong inducement to all our workers to stay with us. We announced: 'Nobody will pay you more or will treat you better than Studebaker. We are your friends. Come to us when you are in trouble and we will help you. No Studebaker employee can fail to be successful if he will stick with us and be industrious.'

"To encourage them to do this we adopted a system of rewards for continuous service. These rewards were paid each worker on the anniversary of the day he or she entered our employment. We pay 5 per cent. of the worker's wages at the end of the first year, the second year, the third year, and the fourth year, and on the fifth year raise the bonus to 10 per cent. and continue it for every year after that.

"Also, we became convinced that vacations are just as necessary and beneficial for industrial workers as for office workers. So we began giving every worker one week's vacation after two years' service. We give them their pay before starting so that they may have something to enjoy themselves with.

ALBERT R. ERSKINE

"We went farther than that. We offered to buy stock for them and let them pay for it 10 per cent. down and the balance in monthly payments over two-and-a-half years. We not only credit them with the dividends all the stockholders receive, but we pay 50 per cent. more as a service dividend.

"We also adopted a pension plan. Any man who has worked 20 years and arrives at the age of 60 can retire on a pension amounting to 25 per cent. of his average annual earnings for the previous five years, with a minimum of $30 a month. The plan expressly stipulates that no management can at any time cancel these pensions already granted.

"We have also our own life insurance plan. To the dependents of any indigent plant employee of five years' standing or more who dies, a cash payment of $500 is made immediately.

"We have thus five different plans which entail fixed charges that come before dividends or bonuses to management.

"But what is the result? *Our men build their very souls into the Studebaker cars.* They don't soldier on the job. They do honest work. The cars show it."

Studebaker has "A Great White Father." The Rev. Dr. Charles A. Lippincott, formerly a successful Presbyterian minister, has a desk in the center of the Studebaker plant and to him the men bring all their troubles. His mission is to help them in every way. He sits in at all wage conferences.

"Since Dr. Lippincott came with us, in 1919, we

have never had any labor troubles," Mr. Erskine emphasized with great satisfaction.

The Studebaker men form a happy family. They have a one-hundred-piece military band, a fifty-piece symphony orchestra, three social clubs, a dozen ball teams, etc.

"No competitor ever takes away from us a Studebaker man that we want to keep — and we never take any of theirs," declares Mr. Erskine. "We are all partners. There is no politics from top to bottom of our organization. Every man eats and thinks and dreams Studebaker."

Although first an office clerk and later an accountant, Mr. Erskine started reading all the technical journals and periodicals he could lay his hands on when a lad of only fifteen and has kept up the practice ever since. Incidentally, he has read the dictionary every day for thirty years.

Success usually is built on solid foundations. The Studebakers laid solid foundations during three generations. Albert R. Erskine personally has laid solid foundations — and built solidly.

HARVEY S. FIRESTONE

PERHAPS no one knows better than Harvey S. Firestone what it means to "swim up-stream." When he, at the age of eighteen, left the old home in Columbiana County, Ohio, to take a course in a Cleveland business college, graduating to the bookkeeper's stool in a little coal office in Columbus, Ohio, nobody suspected that some day he would be a recognized leader in the automobile tire manufacturing industry.

Away back in the early days, when a rubber-tired buggy was considered the height of riding luxury, two men sat at a small table in a modest restaurant in the business section of Detroit. The younger man was in charge of the Michigan interests of a well-known buggy company, and conversation naturally turned toward modern improvements in vehicles, and particularly the introduction of the rubber tire.

Suddenly the salesman turned toward his companion and said earnestly:

"If I could get together enough money to open a little factory, I would make rubber tires."

"The idea is all right, Harvey," said his companion, "but the market isn't big enough. How many people are there, do you suppose, who know anything at all about rubber tires? And how many more would be willing to pay for them?"

Harvey Firestone was puzzled for a moment.

"But I had spent too many wakeful nights thinking over that matter," he said to me, "to let him choke me off that way. To me the market was without limit, because the country was full of vehicles, and every man who owned a carriage was a possible prospect. That's the way it looked to my optimistic mind."

So he replied to his friend in this manner:

"The big profit in a new idea goes to the man who gets in first on the market, if he outlines the proper program. The public can be educated to the value of rubber tires, and it is the business of the man who makes them to find a way to put them out at a price low enough so people can not afford not to buy them."

"But I soon found out," said Mr. Firestone, "that it is one thing to have a sound idea, and still another to put it over. Educating the public to new ways is a difficult task. People had grown accustomed to steel-shod wheels, and the rubber tire was too radical a change to find ready acceptance.

"Nevertheless, my friend was much interested in the proposition. I had taken him out for a ride in my rubber-tired buggy, as a sort of demonstration, just as our salesmen to-day take prospects for a ride in cars equipped with Firestone balloon tires — to prove the merits of the tires as to ease and comfort. My friend was ready to admit that most of the strain we feel from a long ride comes from the jolting over uneven stretches of road. He said he had never before returned from a buggy ride so fresh and rested — we had taken a twenty-mile drive.

"As for myself, I was thoroughly convinced that if we could get people to try riding on rubber-tired carriage wheels they would never go back to the old style. I put my plan before him frankly and candidly, and he finally decided to 'take a chance' with me."

Far into the night the two men discussed means and methods of financing. Mr. Firestone had no ready cash for the purpose, and his companion hadn't sufficient funds to meet the expected requirements.

After considerable deliberation, however, the two men decided to look around for a third party, who might be induced to invest an amount equal to that offered by Mr. Firestone's friend — about one thousand dollars — and if the search met with success the business would be launched. Mr. Firestone was to "invest" his experience.

One circumstance of importance figured in bringing about a quick decision. Mr. Firestone's friend, who, by the way, was a Chicago man, had mentioned earlier in the evening that a little run-down factory in his city — on Wabash Avenue, near Harrison Street — possibly might answer their purpose, and that it could be "bought for a song." It actually had been offered for $1,500. If they could raise that amount, and enough more to start operations, the way was opened for the making of some money.

The whole idea fired Mr. Firestone's imagination, but he was in a rather embarrassing situation without ready cash. His work in Detroit had necessarily put him in contact with several very successful men who were prominent socially and in a business way. Circulating in this atmosphere, of course, made certain demands on his purse. Besides, he had recently married, and the matrimonial venture had necessitated a drain on his rather limited bank account.

At any rate, Mr. Firestone was living comfortably, even though not luxuriously, in a city where he had already established a good business standing. Could he afford to put all this into the discard and start at the bottom again, just for the sake of having a business of his own?

He thought it over, and decidedly careful was he in analyzing the proposition, arriving at the conclusion that he not only *could* afford to take the step, but *would*.

After several disheartening weeks the necessary cash was raised and the little factory was purchased, but when arrangements had been completed the trio found their total cash assets amounted to something less than $1,000. Of this nearly $700 was used to get the infant project under way. They were left with a "pitiful surplus."

Few persons who have not experienced a like predicament can imagine what Harvey Firestone went through during those first two or three years, for upon his shoulders rested the responsibility of the company's making good.

"I want to tell you," he said, "that in those days a dollar looked as big as a buggy wheel, and it wasn't rubber-tired at that."

Day after day he studied closely all items of expenditure, to see where costs could be reduced in an effort to make each dollar do the work ordinarily done by two. Even small items, such as postage stamps, came in for consideration. Letters were written only when letters were absolutely necessary.

The company started with just one employee, at small pay. Mr. Firestone's salary with the buggy company was fairly liberal, but now he had to cut his house rent to $27.50 a month and his grocery bills to a point which would be considered impossible by the average laborer to-day. He put all his energy into building up the business.

You will get an idea of how he succeeded when I tell you that the Firestone Tire & Rubber Company, at Akron, Ohio, to-day has an output of approximately 10,000,000 tires a year which is close to one-fourth of the entire tire production of the United States.

The Firestone organization is made up of over 12,000 employees, and every one is a stockholder in the company, which, according to the last annual statement, has assets of over $56,000,000 and a surplus of more than $26,000,000. Sales for a recent year were approximately $77,600,000, an increase of 20 per cent. over the previous year.

To keep before the public in an advertising way the Firestone tires, the company sets aside $2,000,000 or more annually. Yet, when the little plant was operating in Chicago the partners in the firm would give serious consideration to a proposal to spend eight or ten dollars for an advertisement.

Going back to the early days of Mr. Firestone's venture, the company was confronted with many discouragements, but it struggled through all of them. The three partners frequently had to resort to heroic measures to finance operations. Often there wasn't enough cash in their bank account to meet actual expenses.

It was not until the third year's end — 1898 — that the business began to show a profit. But just as they saw the tide turning in their favor, the manufacturers of a welding machine which they were using made a demand for the contraption. Mr. Firestone went to the president of the company that owned the machine, but was told that the company was legally obligated to take it out.

"Very well," said Mr. Firestone; "we can't prevent your taking the machine away, but we are not going to let your action wreck our business. If necessary, we'll build a machine ourselves — a better machine than yours."

The welding contrivance was removed and immediately Mr. Firestone and his partners began experimenting on a device which soon was perfected, and the work of welding went along without hindrance. But more trouble loomed. The energetic partners found themselves defendant in a suit, charged with infringement of a patent.

More bad luck followed; they lost the suit. To appeal meant expense which couldn't be afforded, so Mr. Firestone suggested that a happy solution to the infringement difficulty and competitive struggles might be brought about by a merger of the two companies. The idea met unanimous approval, and the coalition was effected in 1899, the Chicago trio being represented by assets of $40,000, while those of the Rubber Tire Wheel Company were $200,000.

With Mr. Firestone in charge of Western interests, the organization proved very successful and eventually disposed of its holdings for $1,250,000 to a group of New York bankers, the value of Mr. Firestone's company having been fixed at $250,000, of which he received his proportionate share. The concern was later capitalized at $8,000,000 under the name of the Consolidated Rubber Company.

Although Mr. Firestone was asked to remain with the new organization, he declined, being intent on heading his own company. He felt sure this would enable him to carry out certain definite ideals. He went back to the farm to rest and to think over his new plans.

Looking over the high lights of his career, the young manufacturer found that he had accomplished most when he had determined his own policies and had carried them out along lines akin to his way of thinking. He decided, therefore, to embark once more in business for himself.

"While I was looking around for a good opening," said Mr. Firestone, "I had what seemed to be a rather attractive offer from an Akron company. I had almost definitely decided to go into business for myself, but conditions did not appear to be just right at that time for the venture. But not long after I accepted the offer I became convinced that I had made a mistake. Once again I turned my attention toward locating a site for a tire plant.

"Early in 1901 I ran across an old foundry building in Akron. It was on the outskirts of the town, in poor condition, and really in no particular sense adapted to the manufacture of tires. But it could be bought for $4,500, which was a consideration. I was eager to get started, as automobiles were growing in numbers week after week, and I felt there was a bright future if once I could get a factory going.

"The building was seventy-five feet wide by one hundred feet long — so small that we could almost lose it in the open spaces at our Plant One. At that time, though, the building looked like all outdoors to me. And I made the deal.

"Then real work for me was under way again. My training in Chicago had been in a trying school, and here was where I began to reap the results. I had learned to cut down every expense to the minimum. I looked around until I found some fairly good second-hand equipment, for I had not forgotten what it meant to try to run a business without a surplus. I decided never again to invest all the ready cash I had in the plant itself.

"Do you know," continued Mr. Firestone, "that one of the principal causes of failure is the fact that men do not leave themselves sufficient capital to swing their business operations? Often they could take advantage of a favorable opportunity to buy raw materials or to

HARVEY S. FIRESTONE

secure a desirable piece of property, if they only had the ready cash. To get the money they have to strain their credit, and good credit is one of the most vital assets of business.

"I have always made it a point not to strain or impair my credit. The man who pushes his credit to the limit is taking too many chances. He should always take a little less than is offered to him."

The small factory was the start of the Firestone Tire & Rubber Company, now the largest concern in the world manufacturing tires exclusively. It began with 17 employees. The initial production was carriage tires, but soon automobile tires were also made.

Mr. Firestone watched the advancement of the motor car industry with the keenest interest and with that rare vision which has characterized his various undertakings. He was probably the first to see that the delicate mechanism of the automobile would demand a tire which would reduce the jar and jolt to the minimum, and he conceived the idea of working out some satisfactory form or type of pneumatic tires. While even some of his friends laughed at his experiments, he kept doggedly on.

He knew what he was after, and he intended to see it through. He carried on the most exacting experimental work. And very soon after the new tire was ready for the market the orders began to pour in. Before long the capacity of the plant was doubled.

The Firestone Tire & Rubber Company continued

to grow, and to-day Mr. Firestone is recognized as a dominating factor in the tire industry.

I asked this successful manufacturer to tell me something of what he considered the important fundamentals of his success. His answer, to my mind, was astonishing.

"I attribute much of my advancement and progress to the fact that I lacked capital," was his quick response. "Because of this I had to watch every expenditure. If I had not known or experienced the situation of needing money — where I really had to do some close figuring — to start my business, it would never have grown to the proportions you see here to-day, because I would not have had to study its every detail.

"It is true that from my earliest recollection constructive work of all kinds has always gripped me; and that is a big help. As a child I would stand for hours, watching bricklayers or carpenters put up a building. And to this day the laying on one stone upon another in the erection of a structure holds my attention.

"As I grew older I became interested in the way men started in business, and it was the opinions I formed, and which I longed to test, that so influenced me in starting a business of my own.

"Later on, as I employed men, I found an absorbing interest in their development. When I, myself, had charge of the hiring of men I studied each man carefully, for to be successful in business a man must be a profit-maker, and to be a profit-maker he must have certain fundamental traits.

"I want men who think quickly and clearly, men who have had sound, even if insufficient, training and who have good analytical powers. The man who is to be an asset to the business must have energy and persistence, and he must be straightforward and ambitious. If he has these major virtues, we need not worry about his minor faults, for the latter can be corrected — they'll gradually work out if he is given an opportunity to develop his sound, fundamental traits.

"Good executives are scarce and an employer is often inclined to push a fairly capable man too rapidly. Quick promotion can have an effect just as injurious to a man as a tendency to hold him back. In some cases men are hurriedly promoted to positions they are unable to fill satisfactorily, and they become discouraged — so much so that it breaks them. These very men, if advanced slowly, might have reached the proper heights without difficulty. A man should be properly placed. The employer can't afford to experiment with his organization. He must *know*.

"One reason, it has been observed, why many men fail is because they have no goal. They work hard, but aimlessly. In other words they don't set up for themselves an objective and then bend all their efforts toward attaining it. The minute a man finds himself running around in a circle and not getting anywhere, he should set some definite point which he desires to reach, and then make everything he does assist him along to that end. When he has gained this point, he should then set another one higher up, and so on until his ultimate goal is reached.

"The routine worker, the man who drifts along with the current, perhaps has the qualifications for making a first-class employee or executive. His ability must be analyzed, and he must be put into a position where he fits.

"It's a long pull, and a hard pull and a pull all together in this world, anyway. It takes energy, foresight and ability to pull against the current. There's an old saying to the effect that 'only the game fish swim up stream.' It requires work, hard work, in any endeavor, to achieve success."

Mr. Firestone himself goes out on the road at intervals to help push the tire sales of his company. And he's a good salesman. Some of his friends are fond of telling a very interesting little story regarding his ability as a salesman and his quick grasp of a difficult situation.

Something over twelve years ago Firestone, Ford, and Luther Burbank were having a get-together meeting at Burbank's home at Santa Rosa, California. They decided to visit Los Angeles, and on the way the two business men began to tease Burbank — good naturedly, of course — about his pet hobbies.

The plant wizard in turn started an argument as to which of the two manufacturers was the better salesman, saying he would bet neither of them could sell a thing in Santa Rosa.

"All right," said Firestone, "give us a chance."

"There's a rich old Indian here in Santa Rosa," said Burbank, "and I think he ought to have a Ford car. You go down and sell him one, Henry, and then let Firestone fit him out with tires."

The next day Ford talked himself hoarse in an unsuccessful endeavor to convince the Indian that he ought to own a Ford car.

Apparently that let Firestone out, but he refused to take advantage of it.

"Just give me a little time to think it over," he said. "You've certainly put me up against a problem in salesmanship. But I can't be wiped out like this."

The following day Firestone called on the Indian, and found his small son romping in the front yard. Quick as thought the tire manufacturer ripped the "spare" off his car and gave it to the boy to roll while a conversation was started with the lad's father. As Firestone was about to leave he found that the boy and tire had become inseparable companions, and although the Indian had refused to be talked into buying a car, he insisted on purchasing the tire.

"Well," said Firestone, returning to his two companions, "I didn't sell the Indian a complete set, but I sold him one tire anyway."

Although I did not hear this story from Mr. Firestone, I had it in mind when I questioned him regarding his ideas on the essentials of good salesmanship.

"To me selling is merely a matter of impressing people with certain facts," was his answer. "It is simply a case of using good judgment and practicing absolute honesty in every action relative to putting an article on the market.

"If I were trying to convince a man of a proposition I would try to be certain as to how it would actually benefit him, and then I would put the facts before him as clearly and convincingly as I knew how. Some people do not realize that facts carry weight, whereas a distorted story kills itself and does not bring conviction. I feel the same way about advertising.

"From my point of view advertising copy should tell certain facts about the product which we feel it would be of value to the consumer to know. When we have done that we are through. The less these facts are embellished, the better. Advertising copy was never intended to serve as literature. Beautiful phraseology and artistic grammatical construction are very appetizing to the reader of fiction, but they should have no place in advertising. We want advertising to tell in plain language the merits of our product — to sell goods."

Labor conditions at the Firestone plants had been reported to be as nearly ideal as is possible. My tour of inspection through the company's several plants at Akron convinced me that the report is well founded. There's an atmosphere of satisfaction and contentment in every department. Co-operation and loyalty are ever present. It was easy for me to understand why the Firestone company occupies its high position in the tire industry.

General matters affecting the betterment of the

rubber industry have claimed a large share of Mr. Firestone's attention, and this has been especially true during the last few years. When the British enacted legislation restricting the production and exportation of crude rubber, he took up the cudgel single-handed for American rubber manufacturers and consumers.

Data were gathered by Mr. Firestone, showing that English plantation shareholders controlled about 85 per cent. of the world's supply of raw rubber, and that America consumed about 75 per cent. of the world's output. Restriction meant higher cost of rubber, and this meant higher prices for automobile tires and other commodities made of rubber.

Mr. Firestone presented a large amount of data to the Government, asking that action be taken to combat the restriction act by seeking new sources of rubber supply. The Government took action, at the suggestion of the Departments of Commerce and Agriculture, with the result that an appropriation of a half-million dollars was voted by Congress, without a protest, to send surveying parties to various parts of the world to seek sources of rubber supply outside of the areas affected by the British rubber restriction act.

While Mr. Firestone has a busy business life, he endeavors to see that his life also has a recreational side. A man of intense mental development, earnest purpose, high ideals, and an enormous capacity for work, he recognizes that this must have some recreational balance.

For several years a camping trip in the Summer has

been the custom, Mr. Firestone's companions being men of prominence. On the first trip, in 1916, tents were pitched in the orchard of the late John Burroughs, noted naturalist. In the party were Mr. Burroughs, Mr. Ford, Mr. Edison and Mr. Firestone. That was in 1916.

The picturesque jaunts reached a high degree of interest in 1922, when the late President Harding was persuaded by Mr. Firestone to join the party.

The three men — Firestone, Ford, and Edison — whose names will go down into American history, greatly enjoy these Summer outings, for it is then that they lay aside all serious interests and frolic like schoolboys.

"We get out of life exactly what we put into it," says Harvey S. Firestone. "Life gives back to us more than we bring, it is true; but if we bring nothing it gives us nothing in return.

"Interest, sympathy, a love for earnest work, the human touch, a conscientious wish to close each day with at least some little addition to the structure we are building; the pleasure of knowing that something we have done has speeded the other fellow on his way — these are the things that make life worth while.

"And when you are writing this story," he said to me earnestly, "do not forget to emphasize the fact that no man is important in himself, except as he is able to influence others. Any one individual is a mighty small atom in the universe.

"It is only as we are able to develop others, to bring

out the best that is in them; to guide them to things to which they would not have found their way alone; and only as we are able to receive from them what they have to give, that we can grow and become a worthwhile part of the scheme of things as they are. These are the things that make life complete."

O. D. F.

HENRY FORD

IS the industrial monument which Henry Ford is erecting at such a spectacular rate in danger of toppling over by and by because of its own weight?

His production of more than two million cars, trucks and tractors in one year does not begin to tell the whole story.

Ford has started to run his own line of steamers to Southern ports in the United States, his own line of steamers to South American ports, and his own line of steamers to overseas ports.

He has entered the railroad field on quite a scale with his Detroit, Toledo & Ironton system.

He has acquired his own forests and is operating his own lumber plants, as well as the largest wood distillation plant in the world.

He has purchased large iron ore properties and is conducting colossal furnaces, rolling mills, etc.

He has become coal-mine owner and is supplying both coal and coke to his manufacturing plants as well as carrying on a big business in a multitude of by-products.

He has taken over several important glass factories and is now turning out enormous quantities of plate glass.

He has entered the lists of large-scale cement manufacturers.

HENRY FORD

He has turned manufacturer of auto-lamps, wheels, gears, radiators, etc., on a dazzling scale.

He has rapidly dotted this country, from the Atlantic to the Pacific and from Canada to the Mexican border, with great assembling plants.

He is establishing huge export warehouses on the Atlantic seaboard.

He is manufacturing more automobiles than any other man or corporation in Canada, as well as in Britain and elsewhere, and is understood to be planning plants for every important part of the world.

He has invaded the high-priced automobile field with his Lincoln car and is reported to have towering ambitions in this direction.

He has become a publisher, although here his achievements have failed to match his ambitions.

He has become owner of a large hospital and, over the protest of the medical profession, has set out to run it on what doctors describe as " factory lines."

It is not his fault that he did not some time ago start operations to develop a mammoth electric power plant at Muscle Shoals, Ala., and to become the largest producer of nitrate fertilizer in the world.

He conducts a 1200-acre experimental farm in Michigan.

In 1925 he bought the Stout Metal Airplane Company, sold several all-metal machines to a New York department store for sale at retail, inaugurated a regular freight service from Detroit to Chicago for his own business, bought a thousand acres at Hammond,

Indiana, for a Chicago airpost and factory, announced his intention to establish a network of aerial routes over a large part of the country, began active preparations therefor, and declared: " The airplane is the greatest thing in the world. It is now or never to get hold of commercial flying and make a success of it. We are confident that we can do just that, and we are going to do it." A fleet of airplanes despatched from Detroit to Florida met with mishap and had to wait en route for the arrival of new parts, but this did not daunt Ford or his son — Edsel, says Henry, is the mainspring of this end of the Ford activities. Young Ford and young Rockefeller were announced, early in 1926, as financial supporters of a planned expedition to the North Pole by airship. In February Ford began operating, under Government contract, an air mail line conecting Chicago, Cleveland and Detroit.

The purchase of thousands of acres of land in Georgia by Ford for experimental purposes, including the growing of rubber, was reported in the Spring of 1925.

He is a leading factor in the tractor industry, as the following production figures show, and his intimates declare that he means to develop this branch of his business to gigantic proportions:

1919	45,648
1920	70,955
1921	36,781
1922	68,985
1923	101,898
1924	83,010
1925	104,168

These published figures show how the Ford tree has grown — in output of cars and trucks — in the last twenty years:

1903–4	1,708	1914–15	283,161
1904–5	1,695	1915–16	534,108
1905–6	1,599	1916–17	785,433
1906–7	8,759	1917–18	708,355
1907–8	6,181	1918–19	537,452
1908–9	10,660	*1919	401,982
1909–10	19,051	1920	1,074,336
1910–11	34,979	1921	1,013,958
1911–12	76,150	1922	1,232,268
1912–13	181,951	1923	1,915,485
1913–14	264,972	1924	1,873,581
		1925	1,999,410

* August 1 to December 31.

He has acted the role of banker when the City of Detroit had to find a market for millions of bonds.

How high his political ambitions soar he has not yet clearly revealed. What we do know is that he was a candidate for election to the United States Senate and that there was at one time a very demonstrative " Ford For President " organization.

And more recently, as a side-line, he has undertaken to drive out " jazz " dancing and bring back old-fashioned dancing and fiddling.

Neither our own John D. Rockefeller in his most active days nor the post-war, ill-fated German colossus, Hugo Stinnes, ever aspired to cover such tremendous ground.

What will the final upshot be? One man recently compared Henry Ford to the chameleon of the well-known anecdote: it got along very well until it landed on a Scottish plaid of such a bewildering array of colors that it burst in its attempt to match them all.

Henry Ford, however, has already successfully smashed so many precedents and has so often accomplished what was accepted as the impossible, that he may fool all those who shake their heads and declare that no tree ever quite reaches heaven.

Not possessing the imagination and vision and genius of Ford, it would appear to an ordinary mortal like the writer that there is real danger that the Ford machine will *ultimately* become so colossal, so distended, so many-sided, so complicated as to become unmanageable by one finite brain, even the brain of such a genius as Henry Ford or of his capable and industrious son, Edsel Ford.

Nobody, however, needs to lie awake worrying over any present danger of such a catastrophe. A glance at the Ford finances is sufficient to allay any apprehensions on this score. Ford could, undoubtedly, sell out to-morrow for more than a billion dollars. His profits for the last two years are estimated to have aggregated about $250,000,000, and as he is constantly effecting reductions in production costs, the indications are that his assets will continue to grow at an enviable rate this year and the next and the next. The Ford Motor Company's corporation tax report filed in 1925 showed total assets of $644,624,468, and a Detroit despatch added: " Other Michigan properties of Henry Ford will bring his total wealth to at least the billion-dollar mark, Department of State attachés expect."

HENRY FORD

What has been responsible for Ford's phenomenal success?

First. He was born with mechanical genius.

Second. He was one of the first to believe in the commercial possibilities of a horseless vehicle.

Third. He possessed and exercised infinite patience in conceiving and building a workable motor car.

Fourth. He was the first to grasp and adopt the idea of the lowest possible price and the largest possible production.

Fifth. He finally succeeded in raising the modest amount of capital necessary to start manufacturing.

Sixth. His mechanical genius enabled him to produce a serviceable car extraordinarily light in weight, and, therefore, consuming relatively little gasoline.

Seventh. Instead of extracting from the business and distributing in the form of dividends every dollar of profit, he followed a consistent policy of lowering prices and expanding production.

Eighth. He obtained nation-wide advertising and won the goodwill of labor by announcing, as long ago as 1914, a minimum wage, for all classes of workers, of $5 a day, with the most profitable results.

Ninth. He became a pioneer in devising improved processes of production, including his now famous continuously moving platform which picks up the materials entering into his car and moves right along until the complete car leaves the platform under its own power.

Tenth. He has succeeded all along in being able

to furnish a car at a lower price than any competitor.

Eleventh. Since nothing succeeds like success, Ford became able to acquire properties furnishing raw materials and finished products.

Twelfth. Huge production — and profits — made it possible for him to build assembling plants at desirable points all over the continent as well as in foreign lands.

Thirteenth. His car became the most widely advertised motor vehicle in the world, at little or no cost to him.

Fourteenth. His democratic ways — in the earlier stages of his career, at least — won him almost universal popularity among ordinary folks throughout the United States and elsewhere.

Fifteenth. The phenomenal demand for this lowest priced of all cars made dealers' franchises so popular, even in small communities, that Ford long has been in a position to control distributors and dictate to them to a degree not possible for other manufacturers.

Sixteenth. Only on one occasion in many years has Ford been hampered by anything approaching financial stringency such as has frequently confronted most automobile companies.

Seventeenth. His ownership of a strategic railroad has strengthened his ability to deal with other railroads and to effect quick deliveries to dealers.

Eighteenth. His recently adopted policy of owning and running his own steamship lines is counted upon to entrench his position in foreign markets.

Nineteenth. His plan for enabling persons of modest means to acquire a car by the deposit of $5 a week in a local bank has tapped a new stratum of buyers.

Twentieth. Both Ford and his son give close attention to business and have always had an open ear and an open mind for new suggestions and ideas.

Also, Ford has a genius for obtaining publicity, for keeping his name in front of the people, a faculty of incalculable value. Says Charles Piez, who was prominent in the Government's war-time shipping activities:

" Ford has humor. During the war, he was building subchasers. Mr. Schwab and I happened to be in Detroit, and I asked him if he was ever bothered by the stories which went the rounds about Ford machines.

"' Not at all,' answered Mr. Ford. ' They are all good advertising.'

" Then he told a real Ford story which happened to himself. It seemed that he was experimenting with a worm drive on an old Ford. In testing it out he was driving out into the country some fifteen or twenty miles, when he came to a large car that was stalled at the side of the road. Two men were working and fussing with it. Henry stopped and said:

"' I would like to be of some help, if you will let me.'

" At the end of about fifteen minutes he succeeded in getting the machine going, and one of the men dove down into his pocket and pulled out a dollar.

"' No thanks,' Henry protested, ' I have plenty of money.'

"' You're a liar,' the man protested. ' No man

with plenty of money would drive a machine like that!'"

The story of Henry Ford's early life is so well known that it need be sketched only very briefly here.

Born on a farm at Dearborn, Michigan, on July 30, 1863, he early developed such an interest in tools and machinery that his mother declared he was "born a mechanic." When twelve, he first saw a road engine attached to a threshing machine, and he says, "It was that engine which took me into automotive transportation. Ever since my great interest has been in making a machine that would travel the roads." What followed?

As a lad he became expert as an amateur watchmaker. Disliking farm work because, "considering the results, there was too much work on the place," he became an apprentice mechanic in Detroit, and repaired watches in a jewelry shop at night. He flirted with the idea of entering the watch manufacturing business on a large scale, "but I did not because I figured out that watches were not universal necessities." His apprenticeship over, he served with the local representative of the Westinghouse Company, setting up and repairing their road engines.

Ford's first idea along motor lines was to build a light steam car to take the place of horses, particularly to be used as a tractor. But he soon found that "people were more interested in something that would travel on the road than in something that would do the work of the farms." He actually built a steam car

HENRY FORD

that ran, but concluded that steam was not suitable for light vehicles.

Before this he had read about the development of gas engines in England, and in 1885 he was called upon to repair one in Detroit. Within two years he had built a miniature one. By this time he had returned to his father's farm and was given forty acres of timber land to develop. Here he married. But he later took a job with the Detroit Electric Company as an engineer and machinist for $45 a month. He set up a more elaborate workshop than he had had on the farm and began to experiment with a double-cylinder engine.

"In 1892," he narrates, "I completed my first motor car, but it was not until the Spring of the following year that it ran to my satisfaction." It developed about four horse power, held two people, had a ten-mile and twenty-mile per hour speed — after the motor was started by hand. There was no reverse. After driving it about a thousand miles, Ford sold it, in 1896, for $200. (He has since bought it back.)

He started a second car in 1896, but still kept his position with the electric company until 1899, when he went into the automobile business, becoming chief engineer of the Detroit Automobile Company, organized by "a group of men of speculative turn of mind," to exploit the Ford car. For three years machines were built, but only in very small numbers.

The promoters did not share Ford's theory of low prices and quantity production. So in March, 1902, he resigned and rented a one-story brick shed to continue his experiments. As the speed mania was then raging, Ford, in order to attract attention, built a racer and defeated Alexander Winton, founder of the Winton car, who was then the track champion of the country. Other and more sensational racing records were achieved by specially-manufactured Ford cars.

Then, in 1903, the Ford Motor Company was formed. Says Ford:

"I was vice-president, designer, master mechanic, superintendent and general manager. The capitalization of the company was $100,000, and of this I owned $25\frac{1}{2}$ per cent. The total amount subscribed in cash was about $28,000 — which is the only money that the company has ever received for the capital fund from other than operations.

"In the beginning I thought that it was possible, notwithstanding my former experience, to go forward with a company in which I owned less than the controlling share. I very shortly found I had to have control, and therefore, in 1906, with funds that I had earned in the company, I bought enough stock to bring my holdings up to 51 per cent., and a little later bought enough more to give me $58\frac{1}{2}$ per cent. The new equipment and the whole progress of the company have always been financed out of earnings.

"In 1919 my son Edsel purchased the remaining $41\frac{1}{2}$ per cent. of the stock because certain of the minority stockholders disagreed with my policies. For these shares he paid at the rate of $12,500 for each $100 par and in all paid about $75,000,000."

Ford's history as a manufacturer and as a man is well known, for no private citizen in the whole world has been more talked about and written about than Henry Ford of Detroit. Here we are mainly concerned with his experiences as a motor manufacturer.

His handling of labor has been unique. When the $5-a-day minimum wage was established, Ford launched a program of paternalism and "inquisition," as workers called it, such as no American employer has ever before or has ever since attempted. A veritable army of investigators was let loose to pry into the homes, the bank accounts and every other private matter of his workers. The whole plan — inevitably — proved a fiasco.

From one extreme Ford has gone to the other, judging by his present cold-blooded attitude as described by himself in his autobiography. Read these sentences:

"It is not necessary to have meetings to establish good feelings between individuals or departments.

"There is not much personal contact — the men do their work and go home. A factory is not a drawing room.

"We do not believe in the 'glad hand,' or the professionalized 'personal touch' or 'human element.'

"Propaganda, bulletins, lectures — they are nothing.

" I pity the poor fellow who is so soft and flabby that he must always have an atmosphere of good feeling around him before he can do his work.

" There is altogether too much reliance on good feeling in our business organizations.

" It is not necessary for the employer to love the employee or for the employee to love the employer. What is necessary is that each should try to do justice to the other according to his deserts.

" It will never be possible to put upholstered ease into work. Even when the best is done, work still remains work, and any man who puts himself into his job will feel that it is work.

" And there cannot be much picking and choosing."

After reading these sentiments you will not be astonished to learn that Ford does not believe in charity, in giving away any part of his millions for purposes such as appealed to John D. Rockefeller and Andrew Carnegie. The newspapers in June, 1924, reported: " Ford Gives $25,000 to Y. M. C. A. First Gift to Organized Charity."

But Ford does praiseworthy things which neither Rockefeller nor Carnegie attempted, at least on any considerable scale. He regularly takes on hundreds of convicts newly released from prison and treats them exactly the same as other workmen. He also gives employment to more than his share of " the maimed, the halt and the blind." He believes it is the duty of industry to absorb a share of handicapped humans. He reasons that he can better fulfil his obligations to society by doing such things and also by using his profits to expand his business operations and his employment roll than by handing over large sums for philanthropic purposes. He receives, it is said, an average of 10,000 begging letters every week. The writers, however, waste their postage stamps.

His attitude towards his dealers and other representatives has often been severely criticised. The charge is made that he has been guilty of maintaining an elaborate corps of spies, whose activities — or alleged activities — have aroused bitter condemnation.

Other criticisms have been leveled against him. Indeed, denunciation and ridicule have almost equaled the praises which have been heaped upon him.

Certain labor factions extol him to the skies for his $6-a-day minimum wage; others brand his factory methods as infamous, as forcing men to become mere automatons. He has been called, " the best employer in America," and " absolutely impossible to work with " ; those holding the latter view cite the burst-up between Ford and one after another of his leading early associates, including the Dodge brothers, James Couzens and others. His " Peace Ship " escapade, to " get the boys out of the trenches by Christmas," drew both laudation and condemnation; Ford himself, it may be interesting to know, still regards the project as one of the most worthy he ever essayed.

His bid for Muscle Shoals has been hailed by some as embodying the noblest ambition of Ford's life; it has been interpreted by others as the most audacious effort ever made by a private individual to receive from the United States Government autocratic powers and privileges placing him beyond reach of the law. His proposal that the Government printing presses be set in motion to print paper money to be backed by the waters of the Mississippi drew upon his head the irony and ridicule of the whole financial world, yet at the same time it appealed to many ignorant imaginations utterly unfamiliar with the tragic history of improperly-secured paper currency — what happened in Russia and Germany and in certain lesser countries will at once spring to the reader's mind.

Nor did Ford escape widespread public criticism when his son was exempted from the draft at a time when millions of other parents were giving their sons to the country.

Still more recently Ford's fierce campaign against the Jews, charging leaders of that race with cunning intrigues to bring about domination of the world, has incited far more illwill than goodwill towards him.

Even Ford's latest hobby, namely, the buying of historic old inns, etc., and his collection of antique vehicles of all descriptions as well as other antiques, has not failed to bring poking of fun at him, although why this should be so is not readily understandable.

Yet, when all has been said, the fact remains that Henry Ford stands out as the most popular multi-millionaire in America, as, indeed, the only multi-millionaire whose money-making has not incited charges of profiteering, of questionable financiering, of crushing weaker competitors, of robbing the public. Not even leaders of organized labor or Socialists complain that Ford's money is tainted.

Personally, I regard Henry Ford, despite many eccentricities, which always go with genius, as having done more than any other industrialist to bring about and preserve genuine social democratization in this nation by having made it possible for millions of wage-earners, farmers and other ordinary folks to enjoy the inexhaustible comfort and pleasure derivable from owning that most useful and coveted of all modern inventions, an automobile. The Ford car has been and is an arch-enemy of Socialism, Communism, and other revolutionary " isms." The Ford car has done more to broaden and enrich the life of millions in this country than the telephone, the phonograph and even the radio, combined.

Surely that is no small achievement for one human being in the course of a short lifetime.

B. C. F.

CHARLES D. HASTINGS

"SHUT off the lights, Charlie. It's daylight."

The man spoken to raised himself slowly from the car over which he was bending. He was tired and stiff. He glanced out through the little unwashed panes of glass which served for windows. Outside the snow weighed down the roofs of the buildings that banked the low shed. He wiped his greasy hands on a piece of waste and pulled out his watch.

"Quarter to seven," he said briefly. He stretched his tired muscles, and the set lines around his mouth relaxed.

The car was done. For days these two men had thought of little else but finishing that car. It was the first Hupp exhibition model and in a few short hours it would be shown at the Detroit Automobile Show. With it would go not only their hopes but every cent of money the little company had been able to get together.

But its success would mean even more than ordinary achievement. It was 1908. The automobile business was new. Even so it already had all Detroit in its grip. It was the up-turn of the wave. To get in now meant a chance to enter the business with the first rush of the flood tide. Both men were experienced in the automobile field, but so far they had little to show for their experience. This car marked the turning-point. They were tense with hope and expectation.

As he straightened up, Charlie Hastings sent his mind back over the last few months. They had been full of struggle. Months before, Robert Hupp had conceived definite ideas on the building of an assembled car. Throughout the previous Summer he had worked unceasingly on the model, and finally Hastings had gone with him for a spin in the roughly constructed chassis. Before the first five miles had slipped away he knew it was a winner. Hupp was a technical man, a mechanician; Hastings, a financier and builder. It was a good team, as following events proved.

"Never will I forget the night we finished working on that exhibition car," said Hastings in telling the story. "I think it was the coldest night I ever saw. Working as we were, in cramped positions, thoroughly tired out and continually racing against time, with the wind blowing through the crevices of that shack and chilling us to the marrow, it took all the courage we had to stick. But it was worth it, for the prestige our car gained in the show brought us the money which put us on our feet. Without it the Hupmobile would have ceased to exist."

Every one is interested in the financing of a new company. The method used by the Hupp company was both daring and unusual. The Hupp company started out with exactly $3,500. This was furnished by J. Walter Drake, Joseph R. Drake, and John E.

Baker, Hupp's services constituting the fourth interest. By the time the car was ready for the show the exchequer was practically empty.

Nothing had been concealed from Hastings when he joined the organization. He knew its financial straits. He also knew that upon his resourcefulness in securing money its future would depend. While Hupp worked on the model car he bent all his energy toward devising some plan by which they could raise money enough to build the initial output of cars and get them into the hands of distributors. In their uncomfortable position any plan of financing would necessarily savor of high finance, as they were building entirely on futures, but Hastings' plan as evolved put the issue squarely up to the distributors. His cards were face up on the table.

Through all the tedious strain of the auto show Hastings and Hupp worked incessantly to put the car over with both distributors and dealers. Because of his previous associations Hastings had a large acquaintance among distributors and they had confidence in him. They listened when he told them of the sound merits of the new car, and they flocked to see it. He concealed nothing. He told them frankly that it would be dependent on them whether or not the car continued to exist. He explained that his present plans for financing covered the output of the first 500 cars. After that he hoped to be able to swing the deal without outside aid. Moving among the distributors he asked them whether they would guarantee an advance payment of $50 a car. He sold the entire five hundred before a wheel had been turned in the factory. The money was paid in promptly and as soon as the show was over he and Hupp went back to work. That was in the Spring of 1909. The only other capital put into the company outside of earnings came when Edwin Denby, later Secretary of the Navy, bought in a one-fifth interest for $7,500. This brought the total original capital invested to $11,000.

From this has grown one of the largest plants in the automobile field. The Hupp Motor Corporation's main plant alone has 1,570,000 square feet of floor space, and subsidiary plants bring the total up to 2,750,000 square feet. Subsidiary properties include a factory for gear and machine work in Jackson, Michigan; a large body building plant in Racine, Wisconsin; a Windsor, Ontario, plant for Canadian shipping purposes; and the Detroit Auto Specialties Company, a stamping concern.

Charles D. Hastings's boyhood did not differ much from that of his companions, except that he enjoyed his work. At thirteen he moved to Detroit with his parents from the little town of Hillsdale, Michigan, where he was born. While still in high school he began, as many boys do, to map out a business career for himself. It started humbly enough, working on a newspaper which has since been merged with the Detroit "News," and establishing a newspaper route. Managing this route meant getting up the year 'round at 4 A.M., but Hastings made a good thing out of it and with the two dollars a week he got from the newspaper he kept himself supplied with pocket money, paid his own expenses, and learned something of finance. Later, after he had finished high school, he sold hardware specialties, traveling through the Mid-Western States. It broadened his outlook and he began to acquire a desire to branch out into other business.

Along about this time there happened to be an opening in the freight accounting department of the Michigan Central Railroad, and young Hastings decided it looked like a good chance to get some valuable experience. He liked figures and he wanted to learn something about accounting. The salary was only about $60 a month, but in those days the buying power of the dollar was nearly double what it is now. He not only took it, but he even had the courage to marry on it. He stayed with the railroad for five years, taking on increased responsibilities. Then he resigned. When he was asked to give a reason he said he felt he had progressed as far as he could in that particular line of work. Although he may not have fully sensed the reason, he was by nature a builder and routine work bored him.

His was the story of the rolling stone which gathered no moss but acquired vast experience and polish. His next connection was with a firm of wholesalers, where he was soon made a partner in the company. On the death of the senior partner he closed up the business and at forty-four became office manager of the Detroit plant of the Olds Motor Company.

At that time the Olds company was pioneering. The public, excited by the advent of a new form of locomotion, was clamoring for cars. Profits were rolling up amazingly. Production was the main point at issue, and office methods were far behind because they appeared of less consequence. Hastings knew figures; so profits did not turn his head. He understood office routine; so chaos was abhorrent to him. He had managed his own business; so he had keen insight. The company was moving by leaps; so he saw a chance to grow. Out of chaos he quietly and quickly brought system and order.

When the plant was moved to Lansing, Hastings continued to manage both offices and began to turn his attention toward export trade, which interested him immensely.

"New markets have always interested me," Mr. Hastings said in referring to this period, "and even at that early day I felt that in order to insure maximum consumption we should begin to go out after the trade of other countries. Regardless of home demand we should not overlook foreign markets, for they are profitable and may some day afford an outlet for a surplus. New markets are necessary to keep a product alive. This is true in every line of business. The man who sits down and sells only along a beaten trail gradually chokes his own output. Expansion means progress. New contacts mean new ideas. New uses for an article mean increased sales and a natural improvement in the article itself to meet new conditions. Export trade is the greatest broadening influence a man can have."

Together with Roy Chapin, who at that time was sales manager for the Olds company, Hastings made a close canvass of foreign markets, and the Oldsmobile crept into popularity in other countries. At this particular time their output was about 4,000 cars. Of this number they exported from 700 to 800. It would be a large percentage even now; at that time it was nothing short of remarkable.

About the time the export trade was well under way Chapin and his group became interested in forming the new Thomas-Detroit Company, which was an outgrowth of the "Thomas Flyer." The automobile industry is so new that the careers of the present powers are curiously interwoven. In Detroit the Olds company gave many of them their start, and the Thomas-Detroit was the birthplace of two more, for out of the Thomas-Detroit Company grew the Chalmers and the Hudson and Essex plants of to-day. Soon after the Thomas-Detroit Company was organized Hastings followed the rest of the crowd and took charge of all the work of the sales and promotion department except that connected with actual selling.

It was a few months later that Hastings fell in once more with Hupp and together they tested out the prospective car. To Hastings his experiences had been rich in promise of what lay ahead for the automobile industry. He saw for it a golden future. He felt he would not be satisfied in any other line. To him this new Hupmobile, in which he had absolute confidence, was bound to be a leader if they could only get it through the struggle of the development period.

After the company was well started and distribution in this country was under way, Hastings's mind reverted again to export trade. In 1911, with the company still in its infancy, they sent a Hupmobile around the world to get acquainted in foreign districts. It visited twenty-three countries and made so many friends that its sales future was definitely assured. A foreign campaign was planned immediately and the car was put in the field.

"Isn't it something of an undertaking to establish the sales of a new car in countries so far from home?" I asked. "How did you set about it?"

"Once again I used an already established acquaintance with distributors," Mr. Hastings answered. "A wide acquaintance is of the utmost value, particularly in the automobile business. I knew so many of the foreign distributors from my work with the Olds company that we had what were practically established channels before we even started to sell. My first foreign sale for the Hupmobile was an order for twenty-five cars to be sent to South Africa. The distributor's headquarters were in Cape Town. Even at that time little was known about shipping cars by boat and the trouble we had in making delivery and the difficulty he had in disposing of them in that part of the country came near putting a crimp into our export trade for a while, but we continued to push it vigorously. For eleven years thereafter, or until the post-war slump in foreign business, our export sales averaged better than 25 per cent. of our entire output. Foreign trade is a peculiar business in itself, but it is well worth the study."

Almost from the first the Hupmobile was a success. Within a few months after the building of that historic exhibition car the little company could not keep up with its orders. A total of 1,618 cars were built the first year. Production increased rapidly and by 1910 it had grown to 5,340 cars. In 1913, four years after its organization, the company was on a definitely large production basis with an output of 12,543 cars. Ten years later its output was approximately 35,000.

In the telling of this story I have touched so little on the personal side of Mr. Hastings that I cannot in justice leave it without giving you at least a swift picture of his singularly attractive personality. Men's business principles, in a measure, are determined by the nature of their outside activities, for a man's pleasures are the outgrowth of his personal tastes and of his character. Mr. Hastings has always been keenly interested in sports of all kinds. He is an ardent golfer; has rowed many a winning race; was an enthusiastic boxer. His name is enrolled as a member

CHARLES D. HASTINGS

of the old Detroit Bicycle Club; and he is a good sailor and a director of the famous old Detroit Boat Club.

So keen is Mr. Hastings about sports, travel, and personal activities that in 1914 he decided that his work had been achieved and that he would spend the rest of his life vacationing and in travel. But war loomed large on the horizon that year, and in the latter part of 1915 the abnormal conditions demanded a refinancing and reorganization of the company. It was a situation fraught with the most intense difficulty, and Hastings was called back in January, 1917, after an absence of three years. This was ninety days prior to our entrance into the war. He returned on condition "that he might be released again within six months, or as soon as the crisis was over."

When things were again running smoothly he prepared to take his departure, but as he expressed it he "found himself in love with the job" and by unanimous action of the directors the relation was continued.

The war held the planned expansion back in 1918, but with the signing of the armistice the company forged ahead and in the next four years completed the present magnificent plant at a cost of $8,000,000, all out of earnings. But Hastings was the organization. He was made president and the following year the company earned $3,000,000.

To that eternal question as to why one man succeeds where another fails the success of the Hupp

Motor Corporation offers a logical answer. It has been built in a spirit of co-operation, square dealing, open practices, and honest endeavor. It has what is probably the lowest turnover known, among its distributors. That in itself speaks for its policies.

O. D. F.

FREDERICK J. HAYNES

FRED HAYNES flipped a silver dollar. It is because it fell " tails up " that he became president of Dodge Brothers.

Here is how it happened:

Young Haynes was superintendent of a concern which entered a consolidation and he was anxious to be made superintendent of the larger enterprise. So was another youngish fellow, named John F. Dodge, whom Haynes had never seen. Haynes learned his fate when his rival walked into the place and very brusquely asked him, " Can you pack up this plant? "

" Sure," replied Haynes.

" How soon can you have the job done? "

" By December 31." It was then December 15.

" All right, get busy and do it."

Then, as he strolled away, Dodge remarked, casually, " If you want to come with the plant, come along."

The job was finished by December 30. On New Year's day Haynes showed up at the barn-like building which was to be the new factory, at Hamilton, Ontario.

" It was a terrifically cold day," relates Haynes. " The building was cold as ice, frozen under the floor. In the office I found Dodge and another man, both in overcoats, trying to keep warm around a stove. Dodge's manner was as cold as the weather. His greeting — very brusque — was, ' Your men are out in the shop.' I had sent some men from our plant and I went out to talk with them. By and by Dodge came out. He was as icy as ever.

"'There's nothing doing to-day. Come back to-morrow,' he said.

"I went out into the snow. I debated with myself whether I would stay or go. My welcome hadn't been warm. But I needed a job. Finally, I took a silver dollar out of my pocket, flipped it, and said to myself, 'Heads I go; tails I stay.' It came down tails."

Next day Dodge ordered Haynes to take a gang of men and clean out the place to get it ready for operations. It was almost as dirty as a pig-sty. Day after day Haynes stayed on the unpleasant job. At last the top floor was reached. Here was a battery of old ovens which had been used for baking enamel. They had burned oil and the greasy soot was four inches thick at certain parts. Dodge issued orders that these ovens be thoroughly cleaned out. Haynes said to himself, " I'll clean these ovens so clean that a woman in *a white dress* can sit in them. Then I'm through."

The men thought they were finished after they had gone over the job once. Haynes told them they had only started. Haynes himself worked early and late. Each night he was as black as a negro. The soot somehow managed to work its way below his clothing and he had to rub and scrub before he could go to bed.

Just as the last of the dirt was being carried away, in came Dodge. Having made up his mind to see that job finished and then to quit, Haynes paid no attention to him.

"There's no use you fussing around with this kind of work. You come down with me in the machine-shop," was Dodge's greeting. His whole manner had changed.

In the machine-shop Haynes quickly demonstrated his ability and was made superintendent.

Dodge had purposely "applied the gaff" to find out the kind of stuff Haynes was made of.

When Dodge stepped out, a year later, he recommended Haynes as his successor. And Haynes was duly appointed.

Their ways were destined to meet again. But not the first time Dodge made the attempt. Had this attempt succeeded, Fred Haynes probably would have become a millionaire in a relatively short time. Let Mr. Haynes tell this chapter in his own words:

"In the Fall of 1903, John F. Dodge sent for me to come to Detroit. I went. He offered me a contract for three years, with the Ford Motor Company. He was a director of the Ford Company, was very closely connected with Ford, and the Dodge brothers were making a great many of the parts for Ford's car. Ford had given J. F. a signed contract to offer me.

"He tried hard to sell me the Ford job. I looked over the Ford shop and saw that it didn't amount to much. I told J. F. that if the job had been with him I would have accepted, but that I didn't feel like taking a chance with the Ford people, as I couldn't figure out how they could make enough money to pay me what looked like a very big salary in those days. It was $2,500 a year!"

Years passed. Again John F. Dodge sought the services of the man he had so gruffly and severely put to the test when they first met. Meanwhile, Dodge Brothers had grown greatly. They wanted him to come as factory manager. He went. When the first pay-day came, this happened:

The secretary went to John F. Dodge and asked, "What are we going to pay Haynes?"

"I don't know. We didn't talk about that. Go down and ask him."

"Don't you know how much salary you are going to get?" the secretary asked Haynes.

"No. The subject was never mentioned."

"Well, then, how much do you think you ought to get?"

"I don't know. It's up to J. F."

Back went the secretary to Dodge.

"Find out from him how much he was getting in his last place and pay him the same, whatever it was."

Again, years passed. Dodge Brothers had now become one of the very largest and most profitable automobile enterprises in the world when, first, John F. died suddenly, in January, 1920, and then his brother, Horace E., passed away before the year ended. On

FREDERICK J. HAYNES

January 11, 1921, Dodge Brothers dealers from all over the country were assembled at their annual luncheon in New York during the Automobile Show when the following telegram was received from Detroit and read by the general sales manager:

> Board of Directors Dodge Bros. has elected Mr. Frederick J. Haynes president and general manager. You are authorized to so introduce him at the Dealers' Convention. Please offer Mr. Haynes my heartiest congratulations and best wishes.
>
> HOWARD B. BLOOMER,
> Chairman, Board of Directors.

Five more years passed. Then came the dramatic, historic, announcement that Dillon, Read & Company, New York investment bankers, had purchased Dodge Brothers for $146,000,000 cash. Swiftly following this news, Clarence Dillon, who had had the whole enterprise and its management carefully investigated, issued the statement that Frederick J. Haynes and other executives would continue in charge of operations, undisturbed. In other words, Haynes's handling of the vast enterprise had been found thoroughly successful.

How did Fred Haynes fit himself for so responsible a position?

For one thing, it has been shown that he didn't bother much about the size of his salary. Samuel Vauclain, president of Baldwin Locomotive, confessed not long since that he did not know the amount of his salary. When C. A. Coffin engaged Owen D. Young as vice-president and general counsel of General Electric, nothing was said about salary, and when Mr. Coffin brought up the subject all Mr. Young said was that he must not be paid too much. Many other men now at the top had exactly the same attitude as Fred Haynes and these others — scope, not salary, was their first consideration.

It was for financial reasons, however, that Fred Haynes did not graduate from college. Born in Cooperstown, N. Y., on February 28, 1871, his parents moved to Syracuse when he was ten. Although Fred was an only child and the father was a capable lawyer, the Haynes household was far from opulent; the elder Haynes liked his fellow-beings so much that he was more anxious to get them out of trouble than to get money out of them. The father was fond of mechanics and so was the son, but the mother wanted her only boy to enter law or some other profession.

On finishing high school, the only job Fred could find was in a grocery store, making change, at $6 a week. Soon, however, he found work with the O. H. Short Carriage Company and readily accepted a reduction in pay, to $4.50 a week. Here he made very satisfactory progress. But he began to realize that he needed a better foundation if he were ever to attain his ambition to make his mark in the engineering field.

"I felt very strongly that I must have something

to sell, something more than I was getting," is how Mr. Haynes expressed it.

So, when twenty, he entered the mechanical engineering class at Cornell. He won no medals; he proved just an ordinarily good student. At the end of his junior year the family purse needed replenishing, and Fred refused to continue being a drain upon it. Returning home, he donned overalls and was put in charge of a jig in the Syracuse Bicycle Company's machine-shop. Again his pay was $4.50 a week.

Here we get a glimpse of the young man's make-up. The jig had been so poorly designed that it constantly broke drills no matter how carefully it was operated. The youth explained matters to the superintendent, but with no result. He became so ashamed of going to the tool room for drills that he used to go and buy new ones out of his own meager earnings. Doing second-rate work grated on him. Finally, he went to the general manager, told him he could make himself much more valuable in the draughting-room, and was transferred next morning, at $7.50 a week.

A year later Haynes learned that the Hunter Arms Company, at Fulton, N. Y., planned to enter the bicycle manufacturing field. Taking his courage in his hands, he boldly offered to design the bicycle and all the necessary tools and machinery. He got the job.

In this position he did something which carries a suggestion for other ambitious young men. He sought every opportunity, when his own duties permitted, to associate with the superintendent and he listened intently to the discussion of the multifarious problems brought to that official for decision.

"I found myself," says Mr. Haynes, "carefully weighing every statement made and mentally making a decision. Then I compared the superintendent's decision with my own. Most often he did exactly as I would have done."

In three years (on January 1, 1899) Haynes became superintendent for the important E. C. Stearns Company of Toronto, makers of the then famous "Stearns Yellow Fellow" bicycle. It was when this plant was absorbed by the National Cycle & Automobile Company, then being organized, with headquarters at Hamilton, that Haynes and Dodge were rivals for the position of superintendent of the parent company — the Evans & Dodge Company of Windsor, Ontario, had also gone into the merger.

A year later the National was absorbed by the Canadian Cycle & Motor Company. It was then that Dodge resigned, to go to Detroit, and that Haynes succeeded him as boss of the plant. The salary was only $1,100 a year, but, as Mr. Haynes explained, "what I was after was the experience that went along with the greater responsibilities."

When he reached thirty, Fred Haynes did some serious thinking about his future. Horseless carriages were beginning to appear, and he reasoned that they would cut seriously into the bicycle business. He decided, therefore, that he would seize the first opportunity to branch into a more promising field.

The opportunity soon came. A Syracuse man had been made general manager of the Lake Shore Engine Works, at Marquette, Mich., and, knowing of the record made by Fred Haynes, he offered him the position of superintendent. This company made a wide variety of mining machinery, from hoists to cars, and Haynes figured that here he could widen his knowledge and experience. To Marquette he went, in 1902. It was while here that Dodge tried to sign him up with Ford.

His own company had coaxed and begged him not to leave. A few months later he was rewarded — by being fired! One of the principal owners had sold his interest in the business to a buyer who stipulated that he be given a big position in the company. Hence, the dropping of Haynes. This act of ingratitude, however, did not sour him.

Immediately it became known that he had returned to his home town, the H. H. Franklin Company, pioneer makers of the air-cooled automobile, sought him out. He started as an assistant superintendent, but later became manager of the plant, at an attractive salary. Haynes was holding this position when John F. Dodge prevailed upon him that there were wider opportunities in Detroit. It was at this point — in 1912 — that the little game of battledore-and-shuttlecock over his salary took place.

When Haynes joined Dodge Brothers they were

making parts for 400 Ford cars a day. Haynes was assigned the task of doubling production. He did so. No sooner was that accomplished than he was told to double the output once more.

Meanwhile, John F. and Horace E. Dodge conceived ambitions beyond the making of parts for another manufacturer. Accordingly, in July, 1913, they gave Ford notice that they would not continue their contract with him after July 1, 1914.

Dodge Brothers brought out their first seventeen cars in November, and in the following month production reached 262. Such was the reputation of these men that more than 22,000 firms and individuals applied to become Dodge dealers before the first car was made. Into the Dodge car was built all the mature experience of the Dodge brothers. John F. was the business dynamo, speeding up the organization; Horace was the mechanical genius; Haynes was responsible for production. The Dodge car aimed to combine quality, stability, service, at modest cost. It instantly was accepted by the public as embodying very unusual value. In 1915 some 50,000 were sold, a phenomenal record for a new company.

There were three main reasons for this achievement:

First. Through the sale of their Ford stock to Mr. Ford they obtained an abundance of capital.

Second. They utilized advertising on a distinctly more liberal scale than other manufacturers.

Third. Because of their facilities for mass production, they were able to sell at an attractive price a car that was at once good and good-looking.

The growth of the company is shown by these figures:

	Cars Shipped	Net Sales
1918	85,459	$73,768,885
1919	121,010	120,970,810
1920	145,389	161,002,512
1921	92,476	83,666,248
1922	164,037	130,625,774
1923	179,505	141,332,685
1924	222,236	191,652,446
1925	255,322	216,841,368

Thus, under the presidency of Mr. Haynes there came from the Dodge plant, at Hamtramck, Detroit, more cars than from any other plant in the world, with two exceptions.

The widows of the Dodge brothers had each been left 50 per cent. of the stock. They were not interested in taking any active part in the running of the business and decided, in 1924, that they would sell if they could obtain an adequate all-cash price. J. P. Morgan & Company and Dillon, Read & Company were invited to investigate the property with a view to submitting bids. When the bids were opened, in April, 1925, it was found that Morgan & Company had submitted two proposals, one offering $124,650,000 cash or, as an alternative, $65,000,000 cash and $90,000,000 in notes, to be paid off at the rate of $10,000,000 a year, without interest. The Dillon bid was for $152,000,000 all in cash, minus dividends paid since January 1. The Dillon offer was accepted, and on May 1, 1925, Dillon, Read & Company handed over a check for $146,000,000.

How highly the investing public had come to regard the Dodge enterprise was demonstrated by the unprecedented success of the public offering of $85,000,000 of Dodge preferred stock (carrying, as a bonus, one share of Common " A " stock) and of $75,000,000 6 per cent. bonds, carrying certain conversion privileges. In addition, 500,000 shares of Common " B " voting stock was issued, but not offered for public subscription. The bankers were swamped with subscriptions totaling half-a-billion dollars for the stock alone, and the bonds were subscribed for twice over within an hour.

Could any corporation president have received more convincing testimony of approval of his record than Fred Haynes received, first, by the unprecedented cash price paid for the business and, second, by the public's overwhelming rush to participate in the securities offered? Incidentally, within a few months the Dodge shares were selling at a very substantial premium.

Fred Haynes is powerfully built but he handles himself and the Dodge force of 20,000 quietly. He is not the relentless driver John F. Dodge was; he gets the right kind of results by mild methods. His executives he encourages to shoulder responsibilities. The workmen he wins by his unaffected democracy, his hard-working example, his whole-souled application to the interests of the business — he has never become interested in any outside venture since he joined the company.

Says one who long has been intimately familiar with Mr. Haynes and his methods:

"Business has never hardened him in spite of the tremendous responsibility that rests upon him. He is still as always a big kind-hearted, friendly sort. He has a genuine affection for those who work for him. He actually loves that great plant. In fact, I sometimes think that it has almost become a part of the man himself.

"Haynes is a silent man in a way. He rarely talks in public and seems to prefer to stay out of the limelight. I have often thought of him as the silent man of the industry. He is a dreamer, too, one of the most peculiar dreamers I have ever known. I have listened to him dream a plan until I was convinced that nothing in the world could stop him from carrying it out as he dreamed it. And then, in the fraction of a minute, he would lay his dream before him and dissect it as ruthlessly as if it were mine and not his.

"He has always been his own severest critic, and yet, under his kindly, rather bashful exterior, is a cold-calculating brain of Yankee keenness so thoroughly grounded in his business that he rarely makes a mistake in men or methods. It is often weird to see the almost minute accuracy with which his predictions come true. Haynes receives loyalty and affection and co-operation because he gives them. I have heard him say a thousand times that the only way to get is to give."

Although Mr. Haynes claims that he is a worker and not a talker, he is so full of his business that he says many incisive things in course of conversation. You will agree that these sentences contain much horse-sense and not a few suggestions:

"Pay for good work and see that you get it.

"Give workers the right conditions. After a man is through with his work, let him be his own master. He-men don't want paternalism.

"I would never think of putting up a recreation building at the plant; men want to get away from the plant after their day's work, to be with their families and do what they want. But when they have ambition enough to start something themselves, we back them up. Our men started a gun club. We gave them ground for a club-house and we are sharing the cost of the ammunition and clay pigeons; but each man still pays something. We have no bowling alley at the works — the men can go to better ones than we could provide. But when we have a winning team, we co-operate with them in going to other places to compete with crack teams. The initiative must always be taken by the workers themselves.

"*We don't have strikes.* We treat all our people so fairly that they have no reason or desire to strike.

"We have no star players in our organization. The whole executive organization functions as one team. At the end of the year the question is not, What has this man or What has that man done, but, What has the organization achieved? Every employee knows his job is secure so long as he fills it creditably. Not one man in our organization holds his job through favoritism or pull — and no man can lose his job through favoritism or nepotism.

"I believe in throwing a load on to a man and giving him the full responsibility of carrying it. If I had any executive I felt I must snoop around all the time, it would be better for me to do the job myself. I want an executive to know more about his particular job than I do. If he didn't, he would be no help to me. But every one in the organization knows he can come to me at any time for counsel.

"We insist upon every man in a responsible position training an understudy. Nobody need fear to do this.

"Here's an important point: We have absolutely no politics in the organization. Where men have to play politics they waste half their time trying to figure out whether it will be good politics to do a thing or not. That's fatal.

"We don't have a lot of Yes-men. When a man can show me I'm wrong, he does me and the company a distinct favor. Most of our decisions are adopted only after consultation, and usually an original proposal is licked into better shape by free expression of views.

"Any executive fires himself by doing anything in the slightest way off-color.

"We seldom or never have any legal complications in the running of our business. Corporation lawyers would starve if they didn't get more business from other companies than we give them.

"If there is one thing we take just pride in it is in the sincere belief that we of Dodge Brothers have done something to raise the standard of business practices in this country. Our relations with dealers and the suppliers of our materials have always been conducted on the highest, most honorable plane. With us it is not merely a theory that business to be satisfactory must be mutually profitable; it is both a principle and a daily practice.

"We never take a contract away from a parts-maker who has been serving us well just because some other fellow comes along and offers us the same thing for a few cents less. It doesn't pay. It's not fair to go back on a company that has been giving you good service for a number of years and with which you have built up real goodwill.

"As for dealers, if a dealer has character and capability, the only reason we ever consider cancelling his agreement is because he cannot make money. We require from each of our 3,500 dealers, in addition to a complete weekly report on all deliveries made to customers and an inventory of all cars — new and second-hand — in stock, a detailed financial statement four times a year, and one of them must be a sworn statement. We do not place great dependence on the number of cars shipped from the plant to the dealers; our calculations are based upon the number of cars actually consumed by the public. Also, through a uniform accounting system, dealers compile a profit and loss statement by departments by months, which we analyze closely.

"We insist on an adequate dealer-accounting system — this for his own good. We analyze these statements very carefully, and if a dealer is not making as much profit as he should in some department, we send an expert to find out what's the matter. We carry on a continuous educational campaign to teach them how to make money.

"That they do make money is shown by the fact that *60 per cent. of the dealers we had when we started are still with us*. When the terrible business slump came in 1920 and bankruptcies swept the country, how many Dodge dealers, do you think, failed? Just one.

"In all our activities we try to base our judgment on facts rather than on enthusiasm. Also, we strive to think of things in terms of the future rather than in terms of the present.

"John F. Dodge had an excellent motto which we still follow: 'When you've got to decide a thing in a hurry, don't decide it at all.'

"We know that for anything to be lasting it must be a necessity. Fads come and go, but necessity always remains.

"Our constant aim is not only to build an honest, good car, but to build honest goodwill, and to build it all the time. But to show you how conservatively we have handled our own finances, our balance sheet carried the value of that goodwill at $1."

The day the writer (in 1925) was preparing this article, Dodge Brothers launched a vigorous national advertising campaign, from which the following statements, telling much in little space, are taken:

"Dodge Brothers, during the past eleven years, have built and sold more than one million four hundred thousand motors cars — and more than 90 per cent. of these cars are still in service.

"It has never been Dodge Brothers' policy to build yearly models. When an improvement that is really an improvement is discovered, it is made at once. Their slogan, 'Constantly Improved But No Yearly Models' is familiar the world over.

"Dodge Brothers build one chassis and only one.

"Dodge Brothers have never had an 'off year' or an 'off car.' This is because they have never used the public as a testing ground for 'new models.' Every change has been an improvement on the original design.

"Dodge Brothers pioneered in building the first all-steel open car and the first all-steel closed car.

"Dodge Brothers sell directly through their dealers to the purchaser. There are no sectional distributing agencies to increase the cost of distribution and the cost of the car."

Within a few months of his purchase of Dodge Brothers, Clarence Dillon announced that the majority interest in Graham Brothers, among the largest motor truck manufacturers, had been purchased for cash by Dodge Brothers. Ray A. Graham was appointed general manager of Dodge, and Joseph E. and Robert C. Graham were added to the board. It was also announced that the Grahams, individually, are now among the largest holders of Dodge stock. Graham

Brothers are the largest manufacturers in the world of 1½-ton trucks and rank second in the production of 1½ and 1-ton trucks combined. Their output had been marketed for several years by Dodge dealers.

President Haynes of Dodge Brothers, when not at work, which isn't often, finds his chief delight in the company of his wife and only daughter at their farm, fifty miles from Detroit, where all sorts of uncommon animals, including a couple of bears, are maintained, and where wild game birds are constantly fed and so kindly treated that when Mr. Haynes appears at the lake some of them occasionally swoop down and eat out of his hand. While shooting is his favorite pastime, his hobby is to develop on his estate a wild game preserve.

Mr. Haynes doesn't go around telling people how to succeed. But one little incident and Mr. Haynes's brief comment on it reveal, better than anything else, his recipe for success.

One day, about twenty-five years ago, the Haynes household was going to give a dinner party — a big event, for parties were then few and far between in the modest Haynes home. Fred was cautioned by his wife to be sure and get home as early as possible. Something went wrong with a boiler that day and, although it was not part of his duty, he cheerfully agreed when the boss asked if he would help to repair the damage. He got home at midnight. The guests, of course, had all gone.

"Wasn't your wife angry?" was asked.

"No. Disappointed, but not angry. We got married early, and from the start we realized that, if we were to get anywhere, my job must always come first. That, by the way, is one reason so many men wonder why they don't make more progress. They put their jobs last instead of first. Amusements, social functions, diversions of all kinds are regarded by them as so important that duty often has to take second place.

"I don't say that a man's whole life should consist of business and nothing but business, but I do say and I do know that the man who puts his job first is the man who gives the orders in the end."

B. C. F.

JOHN HERTZ

MY wife wanted to meet me in New York one evening. I didn't like the idea of her traveling in the city alone.

"I'll be all right," she assured me. "I'll take a Yellow taxi."

How has such confidence, shared in every city where the Yellow Taxis operate, been earned?

The story constitutes one of the most inspiring and most illuminating romances of modern American business, a romance of powerful appeal to the ambitious young and of fruitful suggestion to executives and other business men striving to build up successful enterprises.

Like most business epics, it is largely the life story of one individual: John Hertz, ex-newspaper-boy, ex-wagon driver, ex-sport writer and exponent, ex-automobile salesman.

Briefly, America's taxi king won his crown by taking extraordinary pains to win the confidence of his own men and to train them to win the confidence of the public.

Other factors have entered into his dazzling rise, factors such as intelligent efforts to originate a better product than any other on the market, eagerness to lower prices to the consumer, ceaseless search for economies through large-scale buying, large-scale manufacturing, large-scale operating.

But the real, the vital, the fundamental source of John Hertz's success has been *men*.

His success with men has been won by sharing profits with them and sharing their troubles and their aspirations.

Since all business success must be won by satisfying others, the story of how Hertz has gone about satisfying both his own employees and millions of customers will interest readers in all walks of life, for Hertz's success has attained national magnitude — Yellow Taxis are to-day operating in more than 1,300 cities in America.

Hertz busses are already operating by the hundreds in New York, Chicago, and St. Louis and will shortly be serving in a multitude of other cities and suburbs.

Hertz plants have a capacity for producing 10,000 taxi cabs and 1,600 double-decked busses every year. The securities of Hertz companies have a market value of approximately $100,000,000. Hertz employees and their families easily exceed the population of the largest cities in not a few states.

John Hertz is to-day president of the Yellow Cab Company; chairman of the board of the Yellow Truck & Coach Manufacturing Company; chairman of the Omnibus Corporation of America; chairman of the Chicago Motor Coach Company; chairman of the Fifth Avenue Coach Company; chairman of the New York Transportation Company; chairman of the Yellow

Coach Manufacturing Company; chairman of the Yellow Sleeve-Valve Engine Works, Inc.; and chairman of the Benzoline Motor Fuel Company.

Hertz himself gave me a one-word explanation of his success: Courage.

Very early in life Johnnie Hertz needed a large supply of courage. Brought to this country from Austria by his parents when he was only five, he ran away from home, in Chicago, when twelve because his father gave him a sound thrashing — which, he now admits, he doubtless richly deserved. His total capital consisted of the few pennies he raised by selling his school books.

Little though he was, he found a job as office-boy and copy-boy on a newspaper. Existence was hard.

"But," as Mr. Hertz recently remarked, "I was as wild and untamed as the grass on the prairie."

Without any home protection, he had to fight his own battles — and battles with other lads on the street were frequent.

Several years of this kind of life, with little nourishing food, told on his health, and his boss, after sending him to his own doctor, fired him, with the admonition that he had better get an outside job and start going to a gymnasium. Johnnie did both. He took a job driving a merchandise wagon from nine in the morning to nine or ten o'clock every night in return for $6 a week. Also, he began frequenting a gymnasium where prize fighters and other "sports" congregated.

His newspaper experience had developed in him a nose for news and he began to earn two or three dollars a week by furnishing items to a sporting editor, who paid him twenty-five cents an inch for whatever space was devoted to his news "tips." One night, however, the sporting editor (Ed. Sheridan) told Johnnie to write out his items himself. Write for the newspaper! How could he, with his meager education? However, the sporting editor coached him and young Hertz by and by made more as a reporter than he had made as a wagon driver.

Alas, his paper was absorbed in a merger and Hertz lost his job.

And he was engaged to a young lady of good family, Frances Kesner, to whom he would have to offer at least a comfortable home.

What could he do?

"I analyzed my assets and my qualifications," Mr. Hertz related, "and concluded that I had nothing but my wide acquaintanceship in the sporting world. I had won several amateur boxing tournaments at the Chicago Athletic Association and I could see no course open to me except to become manager of some prize fighter. This I did. I was making fairly good money and getting a lot of experience, but my girl vowed that she would not marry me until I gave up this kind of life. As I simply could not think of living long without her, I began looking around for other work.

"I knew a chauffeur who was acting as a demonstrator for an automobile agency and he felt that I should be able to capitalize my friendship with patrons of sport and others by becoming an automobile salesman. I got a start, but although I worked tremendously hard, I made only $800 the first year, not enough to keep us — yes, I got married. But the second year I made $12,000, and the next year I sold more than the manager and seven or eight salesmen combined. I earned $13,500 this third year."

" How did you do it? " I asked.

" Well, for one thing, I was determined that my wife's folks should not be in a position to point their finger at us. This fired me with ambition. Then, of course, I had a great many acquaintances. But, looking back, I can see that the main reason I succeeded was because I sold, not automobiles, but service.

" When I sold a man a car, I was his servant from then on.

" If one of my customers had a breakdown at 2 o'clock in the morning he knew that all he had to do was to telephone me and that I would be on my way to help him out — cars broke down rather often in those days. I bought supplies for them at cost and did everything I could for them. The result was that my customers sold most of my cars for me."

A rich man's son was left a large fortune, but the lady he wanted to marry insisted that he become active in some business. He had taken the agency for the Berliot car, a heavy, $4,500 product. But, after going $45,000 behind, he asked the hustling young Hertz to join him. For $2,000 Hertz got a one-third interest. He was allowed a drawing account of only $65 a week, not enough to maintain his wife and two children; but by this time he had a respectable bank account.

In one year the entire $45,000 loss was wiped out and a $15,000 surplus appeared on the books. But the profits were represented largely by second-hand cars taken in trade.

These second-hand cars became the parents of the now famous Yellow Taxis.

"As my customers weren't buyers of second-hand cars, I had to put on my thinking cap to find some way of disposing of them or making them earn their keep," Mr. Hertz narrates.

"Having driven a delivery wagon, I figured that there should be money in the passenger delivery business. Joy-riding was beginning to become popular. Families were taking to hiring a car for outings, especially on Sundays. And a few taxis were beginning to make their appearance."

The rich man's family didn't relish the idea of being identified with the "livery" business. But Hertz was confident that it held great possibilities. Opportunity to compete for the Chicago Athletic Association concession arose. The agreement called for ten taxis. Hertz couldn't muster that number. But he again donned his thinking cap effectively. He borrowed a few, exhibited his fleet to the committee, and was awarded the concession. Fortified with it, he was able to raise enough money to buy new cars. His first flight into the realm of finance resulted in raising $50,000, the subscribers of which were destined to be the foundation stockholders of the Yellow Cab Company — and to make enormous profits.

Starting a business, like starting a steam engine, entails heavy strain. Although Hertz by this time, 1914, had built up a powerful physique, his health gave way after handling a very bitter strike of Chicago taxi-drivers. The doctor sent him to Europe for a rest. But Hertz kept his eyes open. In Paris he learned that a short taxi ride could be had for ten cents. He investigated.

Back he came determined to revolutionize the taxicab business in this country.

One little incident emphasizes how thoroughly Hertz went to the bottom of things. Having decided to paint his cabs a distinctive color, easily distinguished by the public, he commissioned a local university to ascertain scientifically which color would stand out strongest at a distance. Tests then conducted gave birth to the bright yellow now so familiar on the streets in over a thousand American cities.

Hertz had another idea which was destined to contribute invaluably to his success. Taxi-drivers in those early days were rather hard specimens. And they were harshly handled by the taxicab owners. Hertz resolved that he would not court another disastrous strike. He would, first, carefully pick a superior grade of men, train them to become courteous, efficient salesmen of taxicab service, and bind them to him by paying them well, giving them a share of the earnings, and treating them and their families with the greatest consideration.

Also, he would give the public lower rates than ever before known.

This last problem called for serious study. But Hertz successfully solved it. He ceased paying hotels and other institutions huge sums for concessions; that is, for a monopoly of their cab stands. He figured that if he furnished distinctly better service at a substantially lower price, people would willingly walk a block to call one of his easily-spotted taxis.

Discovering that the cars then in use were unnecessarily heavy and, therefore, expensive to operate, he decided to design and build cars ideal for his use. This step led to the establishment of what has become a huge, profitable car-manufacturing industry, employing a maximum of 3,000 workers.

Nothing succeeds like success, Hertz found. The phenomenal popularity and profitableness of Chicago's Yellow Taxis brought calls from other cities for similar service. Hertz well knew, however, that the mere color of a taxi would not insure success. It had cost him several years of intense study and experimentation and application to weave together a smooth-working organization. He conceived the idea of supplying other cities, not simply with yellow cars of his own manufacture, but of sending out experts to set up complete organizations.

Here, again, he tapped a gold mine. So carefully

did he plan that, although hundreds and hundreds of individuals and companies have started business under the Hertz aegis, the failures have not exceeded one per cent. What Hertz supplies is not a fleet of Yellow Taxis, but a complete business system. Even after the installation Hertz accounting engineers and other experts make periodical visits to search for ways and means of reducing operating costs and improving service.

Most men would have been satisfied to have built up the largest taxicab business in the world, established a large car manufacturing industry, set up hundreds of taxicab systems throughout the principal cities of the country, and to have reached millionairedom. John Hertz wasn't.

"I feel as if I had started a treadmill going and that I must keep on going and going," Mr. Hertz said in a recent letter to the writer. "New developments call for new activities."

When motor busses came along Hertz saw in them an adjunct to his taxicab business. Certain districts could be served better by regular bus service than by taxis. Therefore, he began to run busses.

But just as he found it best to build vehicles ideal for taxicab purposes, so he resolved to design and build his own motor coaches.

Again success crowned his work. Beginning on a modest scale at home, in Chicago, he rapidly added to his fleet and to his factory facilities. New York had "taken to" Yellow Taxis — between 5,000 and

6,000 are in use in Greater New York — but the Metropolis was not satisfied with its motor bus service. Interested parties sent an S. O. S. to John Hertz.

Result: The recent organization of the Omnibus Corporation of America, with a capital of $25,000,000, which has taken over the Fifth Avenue Bus Corporation and the New York Transportation Company, in New York; the Chicago Motor Coach Corporation; and the People's Motor Coach Company of St. Louis. Other cities will gradually be entered, interurban service will be organized, arrangements will be made with traction companies to supplement their services — in short, this field is regarded by Mr. Hertz as virtually unlimited.

Perhaps one of the greatest tributes to the genius of Hertz was the recognition of his position in the truck and bus manufacturing industry by the world's largest motor corporation in the Fall of 1925. An offer then resulted in the consolidation of the Yellow Cab Manufacturing Company with the truck division of General Motors Corporation. From the union of this one-time infant Hertz enterprise with the great giant of the motor industry, is growing a business in the manufacture of taxicabs, motor trucks and motor busses with net sales of $25,000,000 a year and the promise that shortly it will stand as the largest producer of commercially operated vehicles in the world.

Acorns planted by Hertz have a habit of developing into oaks. For example, some 60,000 employees in more than 1,300 cities are operating taxicab systems furnished by the Yellow Cab Manufacturing Company.

Yellow Taxis in one year carried more than 145,000,000 passengers, earned an income of $142,000,000, and covered 612,000,000 miles — equal to 2,550 trips from the earth to the moon!

The Chicago Yellow Cab Company, the only operating company in which Mr. Hertz has financial interest, in the same year carried upwards of 23,000,000 passengers and covered 19,000,000 miles — contrasted with 33,742 passengers carried in 1915.

The Chicago company alone operates 2,800 cabs, employs 5,700 drivers and 1,500 accountants, clerks, telephone operators, etc. Its telephone facilities equal those of the central telephone service of a city of 300,000 people. Upwards of 35,000 calls have been received in one day.

The Yellow Cab Company's securities had a market value in 1925 of more than $25,000,000. Earnings in 1924 reached $2,223,929.

The Chicago Motor Coach Company is rapidly filling its program for supplying 650 busses on routes already mapped out. This company alone employs 3,500 workers and has adopted the same methods for handling them which have proved so signally successful in the taxicab organizations. Also, coach passengers receive the same courteous treatment as Yellow Taxi patrons have always enjoyed.

How and why has John Hertz such achievements to his credit at the age of 46?

He was born a fighter. He himself lists Courage as

his most valuable asset. He admits that he had salesmanship in his blood — his father was a hardware and crockery merchant.

That, briefly, is his own analysis.

Mine is that necessity taught young Hertz to strike out boldly, to cultivate initiative, to develop a faculty for making friends and to strive to give a maximum of service. Then, having experienced many cuffs and kicks when he was a struggling wage earner, he not only realized the importance of treating workers generously and kindly, but his heart impelled him to be humane and considerate.

Moreover, he either inherited or early acquired that which most native-born Americans lack, thoroughness.

"Every driver an escort," is the Hertz slogan. At the very outset he trained every driver to become a salesman. Instead of trying to reform rough-and-ready drivers, he selected promising young men from other walks of life and put them through a comprehensive course not only in driving but in manners, in courtesy, in business-getting. He well understood, however, that, in return for demanding much from them, the men had the right to demand much from him.

And the main key to his success doubtless is to be found in the methods he employed to meet this demand.

He told his men: "The Yellow Cab Company wants to be your father, mother, uncle, aunt, and best friend.

Nothing can happen to you that is not our concern. We have the money and the means to do for you things your father and mother would like to do but can't. You simply go out and treat every customer as if he or she was the last customer you had and you couldn't live without him or her. Do this and you can look upon us as your home. Nobody can put you out of this home without your having the opportunity to lay your case before the general manager."

Hertz proceeded to provide for all his people free medical and dental service, free insurance and free legal service not only for employees but for all members of their families.

Twenty per cent. of the net earnings of the company are set aside to divide among the employees, based upon seniority and merit of the services rendered.

An annual "party" has become a big event of the year; 22,000 attended a recent sociable, three evenings set apart for white and one evening for colored employees.

To rivet the workers still closer to the company, stock was set aside for them, to be paid for out of earnings. Already one-sixth of the entire capital stock is held by the workers.

All this has resulted in enabling the Yellow Cab Company to pick and choose its men. They can earn twice as much as ordinary workers. Consequently, they value their jobs and strive to give satisfaction by satisfying patrons.

Mr. Hertz laughingly says that he hadn't any worries until his stock was listed on the New York Stock Exchange.

"I knew something about the taxicab business, but I knew nothing about the ways of Wall Street," he remarked. "I have now reached the conclusion, however, that the best thing to do is to attend strictly to taking care of business and to leave the stock to take care of itself. That is what I am now doing."

John Hertz admittedly has traveled fast and traveled far in the last ten years.

Now that you know something about the man and his methods, you will probably feel that he is likely to travel a great deal farther in the next ten years.

B. C. F.

EDWARD S. JORDAN

ONE day in September, the "Overland Limited" went rolling across the country into the soft haze of a Wyoming twilight. A dying sunset tore a livid streak of red across the dull brown of the plain. Purple hills etched themselves into the background and from one of the windows of the club car a man watched the velvet road wind out into the rainbow. They stopped at a wayside station. Close beside the track a lithe, splendid girl was mounted on a lean, rangy pony. As the train picked up speed her horse caught the spirit of the chase and sped down the roadway into the gathering dusk.

The whole picture was full of great splashes of life and color. Catching the inspiration of the moment the man snatched up a sheet of paper and began to write. To the worker in the dull drab of the city office he brought the rush and sweep of the open country. The reach of far-stretching plains, freedom, relaxation, moonlight on the open road, vagabonding in Arcady, all were written into the swinging words of his copy. The first lines, now famous, are familiar to every admirer of the Jordan car:

" Somewhere west of Laramie there's a broncho-busting-steer, roping girl who knows what I am talking about. She can tell what a sassy pony, that's a cross between greased lightning and the place where it hits, can do with eleven hundred pounds of steel and action when he is going high, wide and handsome."

Months after, when a group of men were congratulating Edward S. Jordan on the vivid color and pull of his advertising, he told them the story.

Interesting to a degree is the personality of the man who has brought new life into the dull dignity of automobile copy. Racing side by side with Jordan's keen merchandising sense is his vivid love of the open, his vigorous interest in play, his keen knowledge of the call the primitive has for the human, his quick analytical sense of values, and back of it all is the impelling urge generated by his love of adventure, that spirit which keeps him on the road continually traveling from place to place.

Back of the story of this love of dramatic color and adventure lies a tale of early Western life, for he inherited from his mother a brilliant touch of undying spirit. While still a girl she started out with her brothers and sisters, piloted a caravan across the plains to Fremont, Nebraska, and opened a little general store.

From his earliest childhood Jordan saw in life one continual succession of dramatic events. At first the corner of Main Street was the green spot, for from there the wagons lumbered slowly out into space. He wondered to himself for hours what happened to them after they passed the bend in the crossroads.

When the boy was a little older the family moved to

Merrill, Wisconsin, where he spent much time in the adjoining lumber camps. In these rough surroundings he learned the power of appeal to fundamental traits and the joy that comes to every man from overcoming adversity. It was the foundation of an unusual education.

At the age of nine he got a job nailing the bands on shingle packs. It netted him ten cents a day through a long Summer vacation. But it was not work to Jordan. Long before the day was over they had ceased to be shingles and had become a part of the progress of the world.

His next work was peddling newspapers, a duty which caught his imagination because he felt he had a part in spreading the news from the outside world. Often in the gathering twilight the boy was to be found at the end of his route lying flat on his stomach on the warm ground, poring over the news from the great cities which he so longed to visit.

This period marked the first great step in his mental development, for he began to criticize and compare to himself the different ways of handling news and he crammed his mind with the history of events which were taking place in the outside world.

While still too young for the newspaper world he contented himself by taking a job in a plumber's shop which was next door to the village newspaper office where he could hear the pounding of the Gordon presses while he was at work. After hours he hung around the doorway and watched with growing admiration the men who were smart enough to go out and get stories and news. Deeply impressed with the boy's interest, the editor offered him a small job in the office and allowed him to run down news and to write short items. So strongly did he feel this responsibility that he almost wore the tires off his bicycle in an effort to make good.

Nor did his imagination confine itself to the path followed by other correspondents. Mediocrity follows the crowd. He blazed a new trail. Here, as elsewhere, the hardest to get and the most desirable from the reader's standpoint were the personal items. Lounging near the telephone exchange one evening on a quest for news material he caught the idea that this was the center of all the gossip of the town.

No such lead ever escaped Jordan. Soon he made a compact with the operator to give him a line on all important matters which passed over the wires. These he confirmed, and so rapidly did the news columns increase that in a short time the paper was changed from a weekly to a daily issue.

By this time young Jordan had reached his sophomore year in high school, Merrill had exhausted its attractions and he moved to Wausau, where he joined the force of the Wausau "Daily Record." Here he was thrown in with a group of boys who were the sons of rich men, and their talk ran continually on the time when they would leave for college. Most of them were preparing for the University of Wisconsin, and before long young Jordan was wondering how he would like to be left behind.

The day came when the boys met at the station for the Madison train. Jordan was on hand, keen this time not alone from a news sense but with a desire to be one of the group. As he leaned his bicycle against the station platform one of the boys called to him banteringly:

" Going with us, Jordan? "

In a flash he was at the station phone calling up his boyhood chum.

" I'm leaving on the 10:30 with the boys for Madison, Bob," he said. " Train just pulling in. Come over and get my bicycle."

So he entered college life, with $5 in his pocket. His total assets were a two-piece blue serge suit, a derby hat, some accessories, and supreme faith in his own ability to make good.

At Madison he found immediate need for action. He went straight to the " Wisconsin State Journal," whose office has harbored the boyhood ambitions of many famous men, and left as university correspondent at $5 a week, work to start immediately.

On this magnificent income he began his college career. He found a room for $1.50 a week, and satisfied his physical cravings at a three-cent restaurant. Those were busy days. Day after day he hurried from class to newspaper office and then back again to the campus for news, often sitting up late at night to write his " stuff," so that he would be free for class work the next day.

But only for a while was he satisfied with such an income. This was the time of the bitter controversy between Senator Spooner and LaFollette, and Madison was the seat of the news. He arranged a syndicate to serve twenty papers, from each of which he received $20 a month; he was made steward of his "frat," receiving his living expenses in exchange; editorship of his college paper brought him in $30 a month; he was appointed secretary of the 40,000 Club at $25 a week; became agent for the Equitable Life Assurance Company, and later on was made city editor of the "Wisconsin State Journal." By the end of the first year he was making $150 a week. Meanwhile he had also found time to fall in love with a charming girl, whom he married almost immediately after graduation.

Unfortunately, all these duties took up considerable time, and Jordan began to worry about keeping up his college standing. But fortunately for him, in his classes were many men who have since become famous and who even then ranked as brilliant students. With royal good fellowship they kept notes for him, crammed him for exams., studied out the high spots and kept him posted. They also scouted for news for his papers and let him know that they were proud of him. All of which gave him added spirit and courage.

During his senior year, athletics in the Western colleges and particularly in Wisconsin began to show a taint of professionalism. The doors had been opened wide to secure good football men, and a lot of lumberjacks and the rougher element were crowding into the field and demanding money. It was a delicate situation in which the faculty could not interfere; the matter was left to the settlement of the student body.

Soon a series of crisp editorials appeared in the student paper signed by Jordan. These openly attacked professionalism and for a while made the boy a target for some pretty sharp attacks. Before long, however, the majority began to see that idealism rather than rancor was back of the campaign. Jordan made it plain that he had no quarrel with individuals but that he decried the entry of any element into college circles which would lower either the standing or honor of his Alma Mater and that paid lumberjacks who had no desire for education came under that head.

Finally a special meeting of the students was called. Even then the plan was to oust Jordan from college circles. When the meeting was called to order the auditorium was packed to the doors, and a yelling mob waited outside to take part in the fight. Promptly at 7 o'clock the captain of the football team mounted the platform and threw out the challenge that a statement which he had sent to the "Cardinal," the college paper, had not been published. This was expected to precipitate the fight. All they were waiting for was Jordan's reply.

But Jordan was acting under good advice. As the captain took his seat, a well-known lawyer, an alumnus, leaned over and whispered to him:

"Do not controvert that statement."

It was the greatest lesson in self-repression he ever

had to learn. For about a minute there was a painful silence, then by a prearranged signal one of the Jordan group rose and said quietly:

"Fellows, we came here expecting to hear a dramatic discussion, but there does not seem to be anything to discuss. I move that we adjourn." To the astonishment of every one, including Jordan, the men filed out quietly. This marked the turning-point of the movement.

After his graduation Jordan went to Chicago and worked on the staff of the "Inter Ocean," but money did not come as easily as in the old college days and he grew restless. One day while in the editor's office he saw a copy of "Collier's Weekly," wrote them a story and received a check for $500. This was followed by an order for four more stories, all on college athletics, for which he received $1,000 each. On this sum he married.

His next move was to Cleveland, where he worked on the Cleveland "Press" and later edited the house organ for the National Cash Register Company. In the rare personality of John Patterson the boy found a vital source of inspired business. At that time Jordan was only twenty-three and his mind was plastic and receptive to a high degree.

Working beside men who had sifted out for themselves the great fundamentals of life, he learned that to be successful one can be neither selfish nor vain; that the cleverest business principle one can have is old-fashioned honesty; that men dare not think merely of their own interests, but of the service they can render to others; that boys should be made to understand that to love the things they are doing is the biggest thing in the world; that we must forget the comments of less ambitious neighbors, must define our own policies and do the clean-cut, creditable, honest, and decent thing; that the man who has a driving something within him which is satisfied only with the best is bound to win, but that unless men train themselves to their job and love accomplishment they will never succeed; and that to keep ourselves interested and in tune with even the most prosaic daily events we must invest them with a glamour of dramatic interest.

"Men in general are too material and do not make enough human contacts," says Jordan. "If we search for the fundamentals which actually motivate us we will find that they come under four headings: love, money, adventure, and religion. It is to some one of them that we always owe that big urge which pushes us onward. Men who crush these impulses and settle down to everyday routine are bound to sink into mediocrity.

"No man is a complete unit of himself; he needs the contact, the stimulus and the driving power which is generated by his contact with other men, their ideas, and constantly changing scenes.

"There is an old saying that you cannot take from a barrel more than you have put into it. It holds true through all the story of life. We get out of life exactly what we put into it. Personal effort brings individual results. Indifference and selfishness are returned in kind."

An interesting series of incidents, dramatic but too numerous to relate, separated young Jordan from his job with the Cash Register Company, and with three months' advance pay in his pocket he journeyed to Kenosha to visit his wife's people. Here he met Charles T. Jeffrey and within two hours had been offered the position of advertising manager of the Thomas B. Jeffrey Company, makers of the Jeffrey motor car. This happened in 1907.

For ten years young Jordan developed without restriction his brilliant originality. With dynamic energy he wrote advertising copy, booklets, feature articles for the papers, and at the same time supervised sales. His energy was tireless, his optimism apparently inexhaustible, and his sheer joy in every kind of work passed itself on to his associates. It was an enormous period of development unhampered by criticism or restraint. He was a continual stimulus to every one around him.

Late in 1915, Jordan, then just past thirty, was talking with some wagon manufacturers in Dallas, about the future of the automobile industry. Even then the saturation bugaboo was an alluring subject.

"I felt exactly as I do now," said Jordan, "that the saturation point is nothing more nor less than a mirage. Some one once asked Fred Fisher about the saturation point. Fred is no after-dinner speaker, but he is a very successful business man and his ideas are sound. His answer was:

" 'There isn't any — they won't walk.'

"Roughly speaking, it is safe to say that the saturation point for the automobile will never be reached until every one has a car and none of them wears out. When I heard those fellows in Dallas talking about the saturation point having been reached that early in the game it roused all my fighting blood and I said quickly:

" 'If I had $300,000 in cash and a group of young fellows who knew how to keep up sales and hold down overhead I would soon show you whether the saturation point has been reached.'

"There was a long pause and finally one of the group spoke quietly.

" 'I'll back you, Jordan,' he said. 'That's the way I like to hear a young fellow talk. Go ahead with your plans and I'll help you to raise the money.' "

A year was spent in busy preparation. Jordan had long had the idea of a company of his own, and his theories were pretty well developed. He wanted first of all to build a car which was distinctly personal and which would build up goodwill. Large production was not his aim. It was to be a car made from the highest grade parts made by American manufacturers. His motto was to be "Owe less than we can pay."

Early in January, 1916, Jordan resigned from the Jeffrey company and called a meeting of a group of his friends at the University Club in Chicago. He had with him drawings of the proposed Jordan car. He told them with an enthusiasm which would not be denied of his plans for its production, how it would be advertised, how it would be sold. All his salesmanship was brought to bear in this great effort to convince his hearers of his sincerity in putting before the public an honest and distinctive car, and so to organize his company that each year they would do a little better job than the one before. Within an hour $200,000 worth of stock had been subscribed.

With this assurance and a continually increasing enthusiasm in his plan Jordan went to Cleveland and talked to a group of bankers and investors. They agreed to furnish all the remaining funds that were necessary if he would locate in Cleveland.

Actual production was begun within six months and the distribution question was settled for the first year's output by arrangement with forty distributors, each of whom was to take an assignment of fifty cars. After only eight years of operation, the company was producing cars at the rate of ten thousand a year, and had a dealer organization which might well be envied by companies of twice its age. All of his experiences, his knowledge of what life has to offer, Jordan put into his car.

"What of the future of the automobile industry?" I asked this wizard of people's thoughts and desires.

"The public wants a distinctive car, good looking, comfortable, and light of weight for economical operation," said Mr. Jordan. "People get tired of living in houses that look just like everybody else's, and they feel the same way about cars.

"Analysis of the sales of cars determines first of

all, that the natural inclination of the public is first to buy a low-priced car and then a better one. For this reason the dealer who is not farsighted enough to supplement his low-priced line with a better car is losing a big share of potential profits, for having already built up a clientele he should be able to cash in on his early contacts by supplementing his first sales with a higher grade car. Many a dealer handling a successful low-priced line loses his customers as soon as they rise above the point where they are satisfied with the car in his particular field.

"Too many dealers count their profits by the volume of cars sold, whereas a close examination of their statements would often show that although they are putting a number of cars out on the street their actual profits are not large. This is often due to the fact that their territory is small; their discount is low; their service expense considerable; and their overhead as high as if they were handling more than one line. Goodwill established on first sales should be used to a far greater extent by dealers. Once having won an owner's confidence by doing the square thing, the dealer should be able to sell him the second car at a minimum of sales effort, thereby reducing his general average of sales expense, and incidentally securing a greater percentage of profit on the higher priced car. *It isn't the number of automobiles he puts on the street that points to success in his business, but the amount of money he has in the bank at the end of the year.*

"One thing about which we hear a lot of talk is the cornering of the industry. Every now and then somebody warns us that the automobile industry is going to be cornered by some big corporation. What they do not recognize is that while it is comparatively easy to combine oil companies, steel companies, and railroad companies to the disadvantage of smaller competitors, it is not so easy to do so in the automobile business because it was built up by a group of brainy young men, and *you cannot corner style, brains, or hard work*.

"One of the most interesting things about the automobile business is its unlimited opportunity. Almost any moment a good engineer, a good production man, and a good salesman can get together and by bringing out a better looking, more comfortable, better performing, better serving car can take the business away from the big fellow even if he is firmly established.

"In any business where there enters a style element there need be no fear of a monopoly. Just so long as women continually change their style of head dress and the length of their skirts there is going to be a chance for every dressmaker. So it is with the car."

O. D. F.

C. F. KETTERING

ACCURACY and veracity are undoubtedly essential in any writing that attempts to visualize a personality, but by themselves they may fail to paint the picture. Dates and places fix age and environment, but they are not always sufficient to bring the man and his motives and his accomplished works clearly into focus. Most really big men are modest, too, and modesty sometimes hides behind screens, so that no satisfactory glimpse of its possessor can be had.

It is difficult to write the biography of Charles Franklin Kettering, because he feels that he has only now just begun to work to some purpose, for a solved problem is a sucked orange to him, and the only nuts he is really interested in are those that have not yet been cracked. The men who work with him, under his leadership, know the literally untiring energy with which he attacks a problem and the ease with which he keeps several campaigns going at once.

Like many other great Americans, he was born on a farm, and in the State of Ohio. He was fortunate in being gifted with ambition, and in being obliged by circumstances to work hard for a living. The Kettering farm was near Loudonville, in Ashland County, and the date of Charles Franklin's birth was August 29, 1876. His parents, now both deceased, were Jacob Kettering and Martha Hunter Kettering.

It gives some insight into young Kettering's life to know that part of his book-learning he got under difficulties that would have discouraged a less determined personality. But with all his energy and his determination to secure the best possible education, he was 28 when he was graduated from the Ohio State University at Columbus, in 1904. He had been a student in the local district school near the home farm, the Loudonville High School, and the Normal School at Wooster, Ohio, where he entered O. S. U., of which he is now a trustee. Education and practical work went hand in hand for him, for he turned to several means of making money while he was a student.

For a while after his graduation he taught in a country school, but his hands and his brain were so co-ordinated that they had to work together in some creative, tangible way, and he became an installation man for the Star Telephone Company at Ashland, Ohio. He likes to tell the story that he nearly put the company into the hands of a receiver by what the directors thought was too large a switchboard and plant; but he demonstrated, as he has since developed the habit of doing, that he was right, and the company began to make money. Later, he left the telephone business and joined the National Cash Register Company at Dayton — a city that he was destined to help to build into one of the nation's industrial centers.

Every day, into that active brain, came new and useful ideas, and he added to an ability to think in a straight line, which apparently came to him at about

C. F. KETTERING

the time that he began to think at all. Perhaps this characteristic is his outstanding one. He is able to trim a problem of all its branches — reduce it to a trunk — and then follow the trunk line to the solution. Of the many suggestions that find a place on the walls of the General Motors Research Corporation's laboratories at Dayton is one that reads:

"Never mind the obstacles; overcome them and get the facts."

Facts are said to be stubborn things and sometimes the man who knows a good many of them is a bit inclined to be stubborn, too. Mr. Kettering hews to the line; he backs one fact against a whole field of opinions.

"In science," says another of the wall-texts in the laboratories, "opinions are tolerated only when facts are lacking."

And the work of the laboratories is properly described as sifting facts from opinions.

"A fact is a fact," Mr. Kettering says, "and it is always the same; an opinion may vary with what you had for dinner."

Direct speech, always striking, occasionally vernacular and sometimes most vehement, is a characteristic of the man. He can say "Damn!" and mean it with all his heart, but he never swears for meanness. He is impatient of detail. That can be worked out by other men, but no man can plan better how the general principle of the detail to be followed shall be worked out. He is tireless in the chase of facts. Sometimes his associates may take a breathing spell when they are not devoting themselves to some scientific problem — but not the "boss." The tradition is that he pursues scientific investigations during the hours when he is supposed to be asleep; and certainly every morning he comes to the laboratories full of the energy and enthusiasm of a giant refreshed.

He says that everything in the way of a problem is fairly easy of solution, once it is thoroughly understood. So he conceived the idea that it should be easy to make a self-starter for an automobile engine, to turn it over by the energy of a storage battery. This was fact, for him; many others, some of them rated high as engineers, doubted. But these doubts were only opinions. The fact, the Kettering fact, worked out in practice. To-day, automobiles are started by depressing a lever and making electrical contact. They are lighted by moving a switch, and ignition is established with as little trouble. With his idea, he left the National Cash Register organization and started to work out the practical details.

There were delays and discouragements in plenty, but Mr. Kettering pinned his faith to a fact and the work progressed. Problems of ignition and lighting from the same battery that turned the engine over were worked out at the same time.

All this was in 1910, and before the end of the year the self-starter was an accomplished fact.

It had been devised at the request of Henry M. Leland, then at the head of the Cadillac Motor Car Company, and when it was perfected Mr. Leland and his son Wilfred came down from Dayton to see it demonstrated. Mr. Kettering met them at the train, drove them all over Dayton, stopping and starting the car over and over again. It was an impressive, 100 per cent. demonstration. Contracts were signed, and the Lelands were driven to the night train.

When the inventor and his friends returned to their car the self-starter would not work!

But the trouble was located and corrected, and the matter of commercializing the self-starter was begun in earnest. The first electrical self-starter for an automobile was shipped to the Cadillac organization — already a division of General Motors — February 17, 1911. Deliveries on a commercial scale began in August and September of the same year, and have continued in steadily increasing volume since that time. And it is a fact that with the exception of the double voltage device of the earlier forms, the first type of starter is practically the same as the one in use to-day.

Inside of two years it was pretty hard to find a car that was not equipped with a self-starter made by the Dayton Engineering Laboratories Company — shortened to "Delco" for convenience. The barn where the early work had been done was soon outgrown and the first factory had a floor space of 3,200 square feet, with twelve men on the payroll. With the addition of a new building, dedicated in the Spring of 1923, the largest industrial building in the city of Dayton, Delco is now occupying more than 22.67 acres of floor space, in 19 buildings. So much for the potentialities and the practicabilities of one Kettering idea.

Later on, Mr. Kettering conceived the idea of adapting the principles of the self-starter to make small, compact lighting units for communities that were beyond the range of the big power companies. His figures proved, and " Delco-Light " plants are functioning to-day in thousands of remote places. He conceived a system of ignition for the Liberty airplane engines; and this is one of his most important inventions, in view of the service rendered by Liberty planes.

With the success of his inventions came reputation, and while Mr. Kettering cherishes it he has not been spoiled by success. If anything, he works harder than ever, since he has the facilities to carry more and more plans and activities into effect. The laboratories of which he is the active and directing head are 1,000 feet long and 300 feet wide; they contain machinery and equipment competent to make anything from a needle to an automobile.

There are 300 experts at the laboratories, occupied in sifting the opinions out of the facts. And when a fact has been labeled at Research it *is* a fact.

Many so-called facts have been disproved at Dayton, many opinions have been junked as of no value. But as a fact factory Mr. Kettering's organization can be relied upon. The laboratories have made important contributions to the advancement of automobile material, design, and manufacture. The new Ethyl Fluid which is beginning to be marketed by the Ethyl Gasoline Corporation — an addition agent for automotive engine fuel that permits the development of great efficiency; the new oilless bearings and bushings, made of Durex, which require no lubrication after the initial saturation; a new paint, with incredible wearing qualities and durability, of attractive finish, in the development of which assistance was rendered — these are some of the practical things born of the facts sieved out at Research.

And in some uncanny way of his own, Mr. Kettering knows what each of his engineers is doing along about as many major lines of inquiry, besides keeping generally in touch with everything that goes on at the Research laboratories and at the Delco and the Delco-Light organizations. He has lately been relieved of some of the detail at Research by the appointment of a personal assistant.

Mr. Kettering is a man who drives a multiple quadriga of hobbies. He loves natural history; he knows more than a little about every natural science; he speaks without notes at dozens of gatherings in the course of a year and always says things with old-fashioned, homely common sense in them that the crowd can take home and remember. And with all his activities and the recognition and the dignities that have come to him, he is the same man that he was when he walked behind the plow — still the same eager, almost breathless seeker after knowledge that will stand unshaken the test of years.

When the Kettering home at Ridgeleigh Terrace,

across the valley from Research, was built, with its sweeping view and its hospitable rooms, a wonderfully equipped greenhouse was put up at some distance from the house. The school authorities of the neighborhood needed a place for their children to be educated. At the first indication of need Mr. and Mrs. Kettering turned the building over to the children. Just now, the Kettering flowers are being grown in a very small portion of the building. The rest of it is growing well-educated citizens.

Little more than a year after his graduation from college, Mr. Kettering married Miss Olive Williams, of Ashland, Ohio, and they have one son, Eugene Williams Kettering.

A man with a nickname is usually a well-loved man. To his early associates, who are still his closest friends, Charles Franklin Kettering is " Ket," and he is habitually spoken of in the laboratories as " the boss." The contributions of the laboratories and their director to automotive science are of increasing importance, but Mr. Kettering says positively that to-day's achievements will to-morrow be regarded as almost elementary.

" Ket's " brain works in a fashion peculiar to itself. It is a well-established custom at the laboratories, when the luncheon hour is over on Saturday, to have an informal meeting of department heads around the tables before adjourning to a more formal gathering in the conference room. Not long ago " the boss " and " Midge," who in formal life is Thomas F. Midgley, Jr., head of the fuel section at Research, were deep in the discussion of some abstruse chemical formulas and reactions. While the conversation was at the very height of technicality, Mr. Kettering turned his head quickly and said: "No, Fred, that was in 1924," and turned back to the chemical problem without the loss of so much as a symbol. One lobe of his brain had heard some other man make a statement regarding a date that Mr. Kettering knew was an error. So he corrected it on general principles, but without losing his grasp on another line of thought.

Categorically speaking, Mr. Kettering is president of the Dayton Engineering Laboratories Company; president of the General Motors Research Corporation; president of the Ethyl Gasoline Corporation; president of the Moraine Products Company; vice-president and director of the General Motors Corporation; vice-president of the Smith Gas Engineering Company, of Dayton, and director of the Flexible Side Car Company, of Loudonville. He is trustee of the Ohio State University. He was one of the founders of the Dayton Engineers Club and of Triangle Park, a civic playground. He is a member and ex-president of the Society of Automotive Engineers, and a member of the American Society of Mechanical Engineers, American Institute of Electrical Engineers, National Research Council (Advisory Board), University Club of New York City, Dayton Engineers Club and the Army and Navy Club.

And besides all these serious things he is "Ket" — a highly organized and a very human being.

ALVAN MACAULEY

A YOUNG attorney stood by the window of a stuffy little office in Washington, D. C., not so many years ago. The walls were lined with books. In a drawer lay the sheepskin he had won five years before. Papers were piled high on his desk. Blueprints lay on a table near by. When he left law school he had been full of a desire to get out and wrestle with some of the problems which make business history.

What had he really done? Merely worked out honestly and faithfully some of the intricate problems connected with the legal details which had been part of the granting of certain important patents. As he stood there he wondered just how much conscientious effort counted against spectacular achievement.

The door opened and a letter was laid upon his desk. It was from Edward Rector, the senior member of a group of Chicago attorneys with whom he had been working for some time in connection with a number of patents. Alvan Macauley read it eagerly. In effect it told him that his work had been so unusual, his insight into the requirements of his duties so keen, that he had been recommended by the Chicago man to one of his best clients, The National Cash Register Company, as patent attorney.

Macauley was astonished. Of course he *had* put in a lot of extra time working out those patents; but this was a wonderful opportunity to come to him just for that. He was going to have a chance to make good in all the lines which had pulled him. Engineering and law, and perhaps a turn at inventions. All of a sudden he realized that the work he had put in on those patents was not just paid service; it was personal interest.

Before young Macauley had been in Dayton two months it was very apparent that his ability far outran his duties. He had been called to look after the legal end of patents, but that did not take all his time. Every minute he could spare was spent in the factory and in the engineering department. First he learned how to use all the machine tools. Then he turned his attention to making parts, and gradually he began to invent some improvements to the machine.

He went even further. Not satisfied with suggesting the improvements, he worked out his own models and then went ahead and secured the patents. Before long word of what he was doing reached the ears of John Patterson and he called the young man into his office.

"You seem to be interested in the inventive as well as the patent side, Macauley," he said. "How much of this shop work did you have before you came to us?"

Macauley explained to him that he had had two

years of engineering at Lehigh, but dropped it to take up his law course at George Washington University.

"Some men succeed by doing valuable work themselves," Macauley said when he told this story. "Others develop the men around them. Some executives are always looking for native ability in those under them and never lose a chance to help them develop it to the utmost.

"John Patterson was unusual inasmuch as he possessed both these qualities. He impressed upon his associates the value of fundamentals; the importance of living a simple life; the results to be achieved through industry, by doing things a little better and a little more quickly than had been anticipated; and the necessity of giving such conscientious effort that a piece of work was never released until it was as near perfection as it could be made. And he went even further: he watched his men to see whether they were doing these things and he saw to it that effort was rewarded.

"Such principles make a great impression on men who are just starting out. They give them the feeling that honest effort is bound to win. I think one of the worst drawbacks to a boy's career is the idea that he can 'get by' with superficial work and lack of conscientious effort and earnest interest. Another thing he must never be allowed to feel, is a sense of injustice. If a boy once gets the idea that he has put forth his best effort and it has been ignored or overlooked, or that some one less conscientious has been put ahead

ALVAN MACAULEY

of him, he is going to get the idea that honest work is not worth while. That feeling has been responsible for a lot of failures."

When Mr. Patterson saw that Macauley was anxious to take advantage of the opportunities his plant offered, he did all he could to help him. Another patent attorney was engaged to take over his more routine duties and he was placed in entire charge of engineering and inventions, although he still retained supervision of the patents. It was not easy work. Many a night Macauley, then only twenty-seven, worked out the fine points of a new piece of mechanism long after the other men had left the shop. Hours meant nothing at all to him. He stayed right at each piece of work until it was completed.

But all this time Edward Rector, back in Chicago, was keeping a sharp eye on his young protégé. Just about this time the American Arithmometer Company, later known as the Burroughs Adding Machine Company, then located in St. Louis, began to feel the need of new blood. Rector, as attorney, had been asked to keep his eyes open for a live young engineer, and he promptly recommended Macauley.

Macauley hesitated. He was getting along pretty well where he was. He liked the work. He had been successful. Entering on new duties was more or less a step in the dark. But the new company was so insistent that Macauley decided to talk it over with Mr. Patterson.

Mr. Patterson advised him to accept. At that time

the Burroughs Adding Machine Company had only a small office force and a factory roster of about 200, but the machines were in demand and what they needed most of all was some one to push.

Macauley had barely arrived when he found he had stepped into a nice state of affairs. Two cliques were struggling for supremacy, and everything was in chaos. The president and a group which was supporting him were in an open fight with the rest of the board. He soon learned that he had not been brought in to please the president.

The position called for all the tact and diplomacy he possessed. Before he had been there twenty-four hours he saw that the situation could not last. It was no time to take sides. He had no grievances of his own, he was not bound by sympathy with either party, and, all in all, he was in a good position to look at the matter clearly and impartially.

It was a good thing that his bridges had been burned behind him, otherwise Macauley might have returned to Dayton. His first night in St. Louis found him torn by conflicting emotions. He well knew that Rector felt there was a big opportunity down there for him or he would not have suggested the position, but there was a long stretch still to go. To come from a well-organized company into such a medley of conflicting currents was a pretty severe test. Nevertheless, he decided that he had no choice but to stick.

"There is an inflexible law," declared Macauley, "which binds men who have once started to go on building." His reputation had been established in some measure by the work of twelve years. He had accepted a responsibility which must be met. There was nothing for him to do but work out his situation as best he could and give his earnest co-operation to every forward-moving principle, regardless of the individual backing.

This state of affairs continued for a month, when matters were brought to a crisis and the president was dismissed by the board. His services were engaged almost immediately by a competing company and he took fifty-two people with him. To say that this crippled the concern would be putting it very mildly; they were stranded, for the departing president left them with exactly one man who really understood how to build adding machines.

The next six months was the most difficult period of Macauley's life. His work alternated between shop and office. On him fell the terrific responsibility of building up an organization about which he knew practically nothing, and with an entirely new force of men. Often he was so discouraged that it took all his willpower to force himself back to his tasks. Many days he put in more than twelve hours at a stretch. He had to reorganize and reconstruct the entire machinery of the company.

What the company needed was not merely an executive, but someone who had a practical knowledge of the development of the machine itself. Macauley felt that the best way to put the company on its feet was to improve the machine, and as soon as he had tied up the threads of the organization so that it was in fair working order he began to look around for expert mechanics to aid in its further development.

One of the most important laws to be considered in every walk of life is the law of compensation. When the departing president added fifty-two men to his new organization he naturally found himself overstaffed. It was only to be expected that these men should seek employment with the Burroughs, and Macauley was mighty glad to get them. He had been handicapped on every side, but now he was going to start with a clean slate. At this time he really founded the principles which have so dominated all his later work.

The famous principles of the Packard company have been declared a masterpiece of executive diplomacy. Mr. Macauley explains them as the outgrowth of his studies of the situation during the emergency period of the Burroughs company.

"Every critical situation a man is forced to meet during his business career should be regarded as a period of advancement," Mr. Macauley said with conviction. "Every test is a chance to move ahead. The man who does not develop himself by meeting emergency conditions has a poor chance for future business success. It is no kindness to a young man to smooth things out for him. He must make his own tools and learn how to use them by himself.

"No one could have worked with John Patterson

without learning that his own business progress meant the development of the men under him. The crisis in the Burroughs company showed how utterly futile is a one-man organization. Most companies develop their employees through a period of years. We were confronted with the need of producing a ready-made organization at a moment's notice. It taught me, with a suddenness I am not liable to forget, that, if you have not certain well-founded ideas and principles on which to build your plans, you are quite likely to buckle in an emergency.

"It has always been a principle that men will be content and will do good work if they are given fair play, an opportunity for advancement, decent surroundings, treatment which promotes their self-respect, an assurance of continued employment and work in which they can take an honest pride. I made this my basis at that time and we went to work."

Among the men who came to Mr. Macauley from the competing company was a young tool maker by the name of Vincent. He was only twenty, but he was already a very clever mechanic. His work attracted immediate attention and within a week he was placed in charge of development and improvement. He had had no engineering experience, but he showed such marked industry and talent that Macauley had him transferred to the engineering department. Within a few months he was acting as chief engineer. To-day Colonel J. G. Vincent is an outstanding figure even among the brilliant engineers in the automobile field.

He is responsible for the many engineering features of one of the highest class cars of the day, for the Liberty motor, which was a wonder of engineering achievement; and he is well known for his open-minded and generous policies in the conduct of his work.

Working along after this fashion Macauley soon developed a remarkable organization that worked as a unit. The Burroughs company soon outgrew its quarters. Adjacent property was bought, and a plan was made by which the two buildings were to be connected by bridging an alley. Just as the contract was about to be let it was discovered that political objections had blocked the deal. Macauley was in a quandary, but not for long. He and his associates determined to leave St. Louis and move to Detroit.

A fireproof factory was erected in Detroit, and one night two train loads of people, furniture, and factory equipment left St. Louis bound for Detroit. The next afternoon the personnel of the Burroughs plant was hard at work in the new factory. The entire work of moving the plant and its employees had been personally supervised by Mr. Macauley, even to the arrangements made for the temporary housing of 450 people. It was a colossal undertaking, carried out without a slip.

It was about this time — 1905 — that better distribution methods were being adopted in the larger plants. With production assured, Macauley began to turn his thoughts to increasing the volume of sales. Market analysis was unknown in those days, and statistics were few, but Macauley began an intensive study of his prospective markets and thereby founded what is recognized as one of the most powerful sales organizations known in this or any other country.

By 1910 the Burroughs Company was forging ahead with great strides, and one day another call came to Macauley's desk. He was asked whether he would accept the position of general manager of the Packard company. At this time the Packard was making a four-cylinder car, and production ran slightly over 2,000 cars a year.

Macauley was still in his thirties. The automobile industry was new. It had a lure for a man who possessed vision. Possibilities were unlimited.

"We did not talk about saturation points so much then as we do to-day," Mr. Macauley assured me, "but my market study had made me give it serious consideration. To me it seemed, as it does now, that the volume of automobile output is only limited by the city planning, which has never given it proper consideration.

"Fundamentally, the traffic volume is the problem of the city plan. Traffic conditions often force a voluntary limitation of the use of automobiles, for problems of public safety must be considered. Even outside the cities, highway building rarely catches up with the traffic volume and except in periods of depression the demand for transportation has always kept ahead of the facilities.

"The automobile industry is a basic industry, inasmuch as it fills a basic human need. Transportation is a fundamental of every form of commercial distribution. It is the very foundation of progress. Vast sections of the country have been opened up to commercial contacts in the last few years by the extensive building of highways which permitted the use of the automobile. It has been said that it will be ten years before the highways will be ample to serve existing traffic. I do not think they will ever reach that point, for sales of cars are progressing in a faster ratio than the development of the highways. It seems to me that this is the strongest determining factor in the saturation point."

For some time before his connection with it Mr. Macauley had known something of the background of the Packard Company.

Down in Warren, Ohio, James W. Packard, a scientific mechanic and an inventor, had been the head of a flourishing little plant where electric lamps were made. With others he became interested in the much-talked-of automobile, imported one for his own use, and finally built a car himself. Soon his friends asked him to build them duplicates, and a small plant was started near the lamp works where the cars were manufactured. The cars he put out were the old one-cylinder cars.

Along came a man with progressive notions.

" Can't you build me a two-cylinder car, Packard? " he inquired.

" You'll have all the trouble you want with one," was Packard's sententious reply.

Finally one of the cars reached Detroit, where it attracted the attention of a little group of capitalists. These men had been looking for some progressive industry in which to invest and they had decided on the automobile as a fertile field. They went down to Warren, where Packard showed them through his plant and was able to give them detailed information on performance, costs, and upkeep. He satisfied them thoroughly as to the sound merits of his car — and he sold them the Packard idea. They started manufacture in Detroit with a few hundred men in a plant built in the center of a pasture. To-day it is one of the busiest sections of Detroit.

At the end of seven years when Macauley was asked to come as general manager, the car was already well-established but not very widely distributed. Here are some of the well-defined principles stated in his own words, to which he adhered closely:

"If a man has no native ability he is not worth much effort, and his native ability is worthless if he is not willing to apply himself conscientiously and with energy. We keep in our organization only the men whom we feel are personally interested in the work itself. To guide them and give them some idea of what we call 'Packard standards,' we have formulated a book of 'Packard principles' to which we insist they shall adhere closely.

"The great difficulty in business administration is in securing the continuity of policies decided upon. Experience shows that only people of the highest intelligence and most thorough training are able to adopt and permanently follow a policy after only one telling. It must be reiterated and restated frequently until it becomes second nature to the organization.

"It is the duty of a manager to know his men — their strength and their weaknesses — and to use each man in that work for which nature and his training have best fitted him.

"The first requisite of a job foreman or factory executive is that he command the respect and, if possible, the regard of the men associated with him or working under his direction. Our foremen are given to understand that they must look for their own success and advancement to the achievement of the men under them.

"My theory of organization is that a chief executive should not have too large a number of contacts, but should keep very closely in touch with all that he has. We have four vice-presidents, each of whom is in supreme authority in his own department. We get together every day and any message is sent down the line through these channels. These men have direct contact with their subordinates and keep in very close touch with everything that is going on. No order is ever given over their heads to their subordinates.

"Another thing the Packard company considers a great factor in its development is its Senior League. This is composed of men who have been with the company for ten years or longer. We consider them of the utmost value in leavening the new men, because they understand our principles, our standards, and our customs.

"The big Packard factory is manned with loyal Americans and we are never even *threatened* with labor troubles. This may be due in part to certain very definite policies, among them the recognition of long-time service. We were the first to recognize the justice of giving the man at the bench a vacation with pay. When our men in the factory have been with us five years they get a $50 bonus and a week's vacation with pay, and at 10 years a $100 bonus and two weeks' vacation with pay."

With other organizations the Packard plant found itself over-extended through war exigencies. Macauley met the situation promptly. Much has been said about the big bond issue. It was put out merely as a precautionary measure and was retired within a few months. The big "Twin-Six" had been put on the market just about the time the World War began. Macauley felt that a lower priced car would meet a growing demand. The new "Single-Six" was placed on the market and was such an immediate success that within forty days its retail sales had reached $10,000,000. Demand became so heavy that the men voluntarily postponed their vacations in an effort to keep up with it.

No story of Packard would be complete without mention of their wonderful development of the Liberty motor and the generosity with which they turned it over to the government, although $400,000 had already been spent on its development. Turned it over, too, with the name "Packard" deleted in order that there might be no lack of co-operation from other manufacturers. Nor did the Packard company wait for government action; it put through and finished 200 motors without any contract, before the other manufacturers were under way — such was its knowledge and faith.

Alvan Macauley has built up a wonderful organization. At forty-four he was custodian for an investment amounting to $30,000,000 and sponsor for 12,000 workmen. He has always held the high quality of the Packard car as the vital point in production. He has a man-to-man fashion of dealing with his people which not only has won their admiration and respect but has given him a high place in industry.

O. D. F.

CHARLES S. MOTT

CHARLES Stewart Mott is an example of a new type of citizen America is producing. This new type is the brainy, busy, successful business man, willing, while still in the very prime of life, to enter the stormy political arena and fill public office, thereby necessitating the giving up, either partly or entirely, of money-making pursuits.

In former generations government was mainly a matter of politics. To-day government, when properly administered, is chiefly a matter of economics, finance, business. Indeed, the United States Government is now commonly described as the largest business undertaking in the land.

Yet is it not an uncomplimentary commentary upon our common sense that we have never elected to the head of any Administration an out-and-out business man? Business leaders themselves have been mainly responsible for this condition. The average professional politician of the past has been more bent upon retaining office and power than upon securing an abler administration of affairs through the drafting into office of long-headed business men of demonstrated judgment and business statesmanship.

But business leaders are arising here and there throughout the country who realize that there is a wide, worthwhile field in public life for useful service.

Said Mr. Mott to me:

"We business men have been content for the most part merely to rail at the doings and the misdeeds of those filling public offices. We often talk sneeringly of this, that and the next foolishness indulged in by 'the politicians.' But what have most of us done to try to better matters? Not a thing.

"Years ago I gave the subject of a citizen's responsibility towards his community, towards his fellowmen, very serious thought, and I decided that I could not very well retain my self-respect unless I were prepared to undertake such public responsibility as others might wish to call upon me to undertake. Here I was, comfortably situated financially, so that my family would not suffer were I to withdraw from daily business. I possessed robust health. I had enjoyed technical training as an engineer, fairly wide experience in the handling of men, experience also in conducting rather large business affairs, thus, presumably, fitting me to some extent at least for dealing with many of the duties connected with administration of civic and state affairs.

"It was because I had reasoned things out in this way and had reached a definite decision that it was incumbent upon me, if I desired to retain in the fullest degree my self-respect, to respond, when possible, to any call that might be made upon me to discharge public duties, that I consented to become mayor of my town years ago, when the people were clamoring to be delivered from the unpleasant conditions brought about by a Socialistic mayor.

"It was in exactly the same spirit that I later consented to allow my name to be put up at the primary election as a candidate for governor of the State. The fact that I did not head the poll did not — could not — alter my carefully-reasoned-out attitude towards the shouldering of public responsibilities whenever called upon to do so.

"America has afforded me opportunity to make reasonable headway in the world and to provide for my family. Why should I not stand ready, like a loyal soldier — I served six years in the Naval Militia and through the Spanish War in the Navy — to take orders from my fellow-citizens and obey any summons to serve to my country in any capacity they might consider me fit to undertake?"

Straightforward, manly, public-spirited talk, is it not?

Outside of his own State and his own industry Charles S. Mott is not very widely known, largely because he is no seeker after publicity, no courter of the limelight. He is, and always has been, a doer rather than a talker. His brain works better than his tongue. He is not a glib orator. He is content to be simply himself — an undemonstrative, serious-minded, hard-working citizen, intent upon getting worthwhile things done efficiently, smoothly, expeditiously, leaving the results to speak for themselves.

General Motors has its financial headquarters in New York, but its operating activities center around Detroit and in other parts of Michigan. C. S. Mott has always been high in the operating counsels of General Motors. It is to him that his fellow-directors and his fellow-members of the executive committee look for unfailing co-operation in guiding and directing the operations of the various huge automobile and other plants that form General Motors.

I doubt whether most people have the faintest conception of the magnitude of the General Motors Corporation of to-day. General Motors in its magnitude is one of the marvels of the modern industrial world. Ponder these facts and figures:

Its total assets exceed $700,000,000.

Its capital stock approximates $750,000,000.

Its net sales in 1925 amounted to well over $725,000,000. It exported more than 100,000 cars at a value of over $75,000,000.

There are more than 60 members of the General Motors family, meaning subsidiary and affiliated companies, all contributing to motor production and distribution.

It has plants located in 35 cities in the United States and Canada.

It maintains merchandising and assembly plants in England, Denmark, Belgium, Argentina, Brazil, Spain, Germany and France. New assembly plants have been established in Wellington, New Zealand and Port Elizabeth, South Africa. These are in addition to the numerous offices of the General Motors Export Company.

It acquired, in November, 1925, a controlling interest in Vauxhall Motors, Ltd., of Luton, England.

It occupies more than 1,500 buildings, covering more than 2,000 acres of land.

It utilizes a total floor space of 35,000,000 square feet.

It makes one of every six motor cars in the United States to-day.

It has turned out 45,000 cars a month, equal to 1,730 cars every day, or 18 cars every five minutes of an eight-hour day.

Its employees aggregate 80,000, exclusive of certain affiliated companies and not counting dealers or service men.

It has 70,000 stockholders.

Behind it are the greatest banking house in the world to-day — J. P. Morgan & Company — and one of the ablest and most successful industrial families in America — the duPonts.

It has a Research division under the direction of C. F. Kettering, "The Edison of the motor industry."

It has an Acceptance Corporation to finance domestic and foreign sales which handles upwards of $200,000,000 of business a year.

It has two Housing Corporations to look after the providing of housing for employees.

It has an Exchange Corporation to handle its insurance brokerage and such-like business.

It owns the largest office building of any industrial corporation in the world.

This building, located in the geographical center of Detroit, but away from the downtown congestion, has 1,700 offices, accommodates 6,000 people, weighs 230,000 tons, has 30 acres of floor space, 5,148 windows, 5,000 radiators, 27 passenger elevators, and was built to endure at least 200 years.

From this building, the center of the Corporation's operating executive activities, C. S. Mott is in close and intimate touch with the operations of such gigantic automobile plants as the Buick, Chevrolet, Cadillac, Oakland, Oldsmobile, GMC Truck, and multifarious affiliated plants, such as Fisher Body, the largest maker of automobile bodies in the world, whose growth within a few years from a small enterprise to a $50,000,000 corporation, constitutes an amazing modern industrial romance.

How successfully General Motors Corporation is now being directed by Alfred P. Sloan, Jr., and his duPont associates, can be gathered from the fact that, after paying $25,000,000 in dividends on the common stock in 1924, and making provision for the regular quarterly dividends on the preferred and the debenture stocks, the surplus at the end of that year exceeded $80,000,000. This was followed by dividend disbursements of more than $45,000,000 in 1925.

How came Mr. Mott to fit himself for the position he now occupies?

He must have been born with a taste for engineering.

CHARLES S. MOTT

(Also, parenthetically, with a taste for patriotic service.) After attending school in Newark, N. J., — where he was born on June 2, 1875 — and in New York City, he attended Stevens High School at Hoboken, N. J., where they give special attention to training youths for entering Stevens Institute of Technology. When nineteen he joined the Naval Militia of the State of New York, and rose to be Chief Gunner's Mate. He amplified his domestic education by studying zymotechnology at Copenhagen for one year and chemistry at Munich for another year. He had little difficulty, therefore, in winning from Stevens Institute the degree of Mechanical Engineer, in 1897.

He hadn't been at work twelve months, with his father, a manufacturer of soda-water apparatus in New York City, when the Spanish-American War broke out, and he promptly volunteered for service in the U. S. Navy. He served as Gunner's Mate, first class, on the U. S. S. "Yankee" in Cuban waters, and was credited with participating in engagements at Cienfuegos, Casilla and Santiago.

A year after young Mott returned to the family firm of C. S. Mott & Company the father died, and C. S. looked around for a wider field, one offering greater scope for his engineering talents. The Weston-Mott Company was manufacturing wire wheels and rims for bicycles, carriages and other vehicles at Utica, N. Y., and the young man decided to throw in his lot there.

Mott immediately took charge of all shop and engineering operations. About this time the bicycle craze died down with the advent of motor cars, and the business threatened to encounter hard times. Young Mott, however, promptly started making axles for automobiles, and he made them so well that the demand steadily increased. He was now (1904) made president, although he was not yet thirty. He had developed not merely into an alert engineer and designer, but into a business-getter and successful handler of men. In addition to doing all the purchasing, he personally sold the entire output, and also acted as treasurer after the death of his associate, W. G. Doolittle, in 1908. He worked unceasingly.

Michigan was then rapidly coming to the front as the home of automobile manufacturing. As more and more of Weston-Mott's output was absorbed by makers of motor cars, Mott conducted investigations and decided that Flint, then a small town, was the ideal center from which to distribute his axles, hubs and rims. Flint was within convenient shipping distance not only of the automobile plants which were springing up in Michigan, but of those being established in Ohio and Illinois.

This move was made in 1906, after repeated additions to the old plant had failed to keep abreast of the requirements. In the new Weston-Mott works the most up-to-date construction possible was used, so that materials were handled efficiently from the moment they were received until they were shipped out as finished products.

CHARLES S. MOTT

Inside of four years the new plant had grown until it employed 2,300 men. Up to this time Mr. Mott had acted as general manager, sales manager and chief engineer himself. He found joy in building up the greatest business of its kind in the country, and it was no hardship for him to work overtime. But he realized that he could accomplish bigger things if he developed other men to shoulder responsibilities. So, as Mr. Mott expressed it to me, " I began organizing myself out of a job."

One of his brightest young men, Harry Bassett, was trained to become factory manager and, later, general manager — this same Harry Bassett is to-day president of the Buick company. A brainy young bookkeeper, Harvey I. Mallery, was developed into the treasurer.

From a concern worth perhaps $100,000 when Mott joined it in 1900, Weston-Mott had grown so rapidly and so soundly that by 1913 it was worth fully $3,000,000 — a very substantial return for thirteen years of intense application.

Meanwhile a transformation was under way in the ownership of automobile-building companies. General Motors, originally formed in 1908, was acquiring control of one after another of the large users of Weston-Mott products. Mr. Mott had held nearly all the stock of his company, but he had parted with 49 per cent. of it to General Motors as this combination took a greater and greater percentage of his output. When it reached the point where Weston-Mott was doing 60 per cent. of its business with General Motors, Mr. Mott consented to exchange his majority holdings for General Motors stock on such terms that the purchasing company didn't have to pay out a single dollar of cash, but earned the full amount from the profits of this new subsidiary.

But it turned out quite as profitably for Mr. Mott. He acquired a block of General Motors stock, both common and preferred, and he added extensively to his holdings, for he had infinite faith in the future of General Motors. In due time he received, in common with all the other stockholders, first, five shares for each of his original shares, and, later, ten shares for each of the five shares, thus multiplying his original number of shares fifty times!

But the deal did more for Mr. Mott than merely make him well-off financially for the rest of his life. Although he soon became a director of General Motors, and was, among various other things, president of the Industrial Savings Bank of Flint (which he had helped to organize to stimulate saving among the working classes), a director of the Genesee County Savings Bank, and secretary-treasurer of the Flint Sandstone Brick Company, he found himself relatively foot-free, and in a position to devote himself to public service.

He became mayor of Flint, served two consecutive terms, again accepted office in 1918, and served until the United States Government called upon him for further patriotic service in connection with straightening out a very serious tangle caused by confusion in the purchase of automotive supplies. He did a good job at Washington — another specimen of direct public service.

When he was mayor of Flint he did things in a businesslike way. He gave Flint up-to-date and adequate sewers, street paving, sidewalks, fire department, financing plans, accounting system, etc.

A loving cup presented to him by his fellow-citizens of Flint bears this inscription: " In grateful recognition of his unselfish devotion to the public weal, his strikingly successful efforts in the direction of city beautification and betterment, his insistence upon the application of business principles and economies in municipal government, and his consistent furtherance of exalted ideals in civic life."

While he was sojourning in California in 1920 a movement was launched to induce Mr. Mott to enter the primaries as a gubernatorial candidate. Although without the backing of any political machine and without opportunity for conducting any State-wide campaign, Mr. Mott ran third among the nine candidates. The machine politicians dubbed him a representative of Big Business, and conjured up alarming pictures of what he would do to the working classes if elected governor. Yet the workers who knew him best — those of Flint, where he had been one of the largest employers for years — voted enthusiastically for him. In his own county (Genesee) he polled more than 10,000 out of 16,000 votes. During this campaign an extraordinary tribute was paid him; fully 10,000 people flocked to his house one evening to cheer him and express their endorsement of the clean-cut principles and policies he champions.

It was natural that Mr. Mott should eagerly give the best in him to unselfish, non-mercenary war work. The Government found itself seriously handicapped by the confusion and needless competition caused by four or five different army corps clamoring, each for itself, for motor vehicles. The Air Corps, the Quartermaster Corps, the Medical Corps, the Ordnance Corps, were making independent and often contradictory and impossible demands upon motor plants. Chaos ruled.

Mr. Mott was installed as Major, Q.M.C., at Detroit, in charge of production of U. S. Army vehicles in the States of Michigan and Indiana. In developing his organization of assistants he drafted from the automobile industry production men fully qualified to perform the functions expected of them. He placed a trusted aid in each plant to check the work turned out. Hitches arising from scarcity of material or other causes were reported and, as he modestly expressed it to me, " All that was necessary was to select the right man to disentangle tangles and get done the things needed to be done. Experience had acquainted me with the ablest men in each branch of the motor industry, so it was easy to pick the right men. I should add that I never had a single call refused; the men in the motor industry responded most patriotically."

Mr. Mott somehow found time for other war work.

Among other things, he was chairman of the Red Cross, and here is one sample of the businesslike efficiency he introduced into everything he became associated with: He found Red Cross workers spending a great deal of time tearing up bandages, so he procured two machines which did the work of scores of women. He also led Liberty Loan drives, and his standing with the working classes enabled him to enlist unusually enthusiastic and widespread support.

The war over, Mr. Mott went to Europe in the Fall of 1919 along with half-a-dozen other General Motors men to inspect automobile plants in France, Italy and England. He was at home in such a capacity, as, in addition to his engineering knowledge, he had inspected many European plants several years before when the Society of Automobile Engineers visited Europe.

From the time he sold out to General Motors, Mr. Mott, although first a director and later a vice-president, had not devoted himself actively to the latter company's affairs. But when W. C. Durant's controlling interest was taken over by the duPonts, in 1921, it was found essential to place someone in charge at the Detroit headquarters to assist in co-ordinating activities in the different plants and to handle problems of personnel.

Influenced largely by his long-time, intimate assosociation with Alfred P. Sloan, Jr., who had become a member of the General Motors Executive Committee in New York, Mr. Mott consented to put his shoulder to the wheel, at least until the mighty industrial Leviathan was steered into smooth seas. In the middle of November he was made a member of the executive committee.

I tried to get Mr. Mott to tell how a man can best cultivate executive qualities. But Mr. Mott is a poor talker about himself or his achievements. With much prodding, I did succeed in getting this much out of him:

"The first consideration in business is to see to it that you produce something for which there is a demand.

"The next thing is to make the thing right, and the next — as important as any — is to make the price right.

"You must exercise eternal vigilance in watching overhead. Many little expenses run into a large sum in the end. Some concerns concentrate almost wholly upon reducing production costs and neglect selling costs. Economic distribution is just as essential as economic production.

"Get facts. Never guess. Keep complete statistical records. Know every month exactly what your business has done in all its departments. Don't merely have these statistics compiled: study them, analyze them, use them as a basis for your reasoning, as a foundation for your vision of the future and your planning. Get down to the bedrock of things. Investigate things to the bottom. Think things through.

"Devote careful attention to training other men to shoulder and properly discharge responsibilities. When you get towards the top, or to the top, organize yourself out of a job. Encourage your best co-workers to reach out for greater responsibilities.

"Don't look over others' shoulders every moment of the day to see what they are doing. Give them scope. Give them latitude. Encourage them to think for themselves. Encourage them to develop initiative. Don't pounce on them when they make mistakes; sit down and reason things out with them so that, while they won't make the same mistake again, they won't be afraid to exercise originality again lest they might make another mistake."

Mr. Mott's countenance radiates health. I touched upon this.

"Yes," he said, "I am a great believer in keeping physically fit. I think this is of tremendous importance for any man who is in earnest about accomplishing the very most of which he is capable.

"I go in for horse-back riding, for farming, for hunting, for fishing whenever I can contrive to find the time. But I don't take vacations to do these things. I believe a man can keep himself in better condition while working and sticking to his job than when he goes away on a vacation and does nothing else but pursue recreation and amusement and exercise. After such a vacation, there comes a relapse. Instead of taking an overdose of exercise for a week or two at a time and then taking little or no real exercise for weeks or months at a stretch, it is better, I believe, to stick right to one's job and squeeze in a rational amount of exercise and recreation right along. This keeps the muscles as well as the mind in condition regularly. It flattens out the health curve, so to speak, instead of sending it away up one week and then letting it slump."

I asked a business man who has been closely associated with Mr. Mott for many years to account for Mr. Mott's notable rise, and this was his reply: "To begin with, he had the foundation of a thorough engineering training. He added to that engineering experience. He combines with his technical knowledge, an extraordinarily keen business sense. He never loses sight of what a thing will cost and what price it will bring. He has vision, yet is no impractical theorist. He always keeps his feet on the ground. He is an analyst through and through. He is a glutton for information, for facts and figures. He scrutinizes costs mercilessly.

"Then, he has almost uncanny judgment. His foresight is as good as most men's hindsight. He is a thinker as well as a doer."

Mr. Mallery related this incident to me: "When I was in charge of the Weston-Mott bookkeeping, one of my duties was to record every month the exact state of affairs in a book which Mr. Mott kept in his own desk and which I had strict injunctions to keep up to the minute. Once when Mr. Mott was away I was so busy that I delayed entering the figures and

Mr. Mott returned. He put his hand into the drawer for the book and, when he found it wasn't there, he immediately summoned me and gave me a laying-out. He told me that I had no business to remove the book from his desk as he might have shown up some evening and wanted the book right away. Then, when he found that I hadn't even then posted the latest figures, he told me never to let such a thing occur again, as he didn't care to read ancient history. I well recall that he added, ' I had enough ancient history at school to last me a lifetime.' "

I have already recorded that Mr. Mott isn't of the " regular fellow," " good mixer " type. Indeed, he gives strangers the impression of being rather austere, unbending, even cold. Yet I discovered, in the course of my investigations, that Mr. Mott, as one of his intimates put it, " has a heart as big as an ox." He gives a great deal of money to the Flint Y. M. C. A. (of which he has been president), to community chests, to the church, to philanthropic societies, and to other worthy or public purposes. But he does it so quietly that few people catch a glimpse of this side of his character.

Many years ago a young man employed by Mr. Mott went to him and explained that he had recently been married and that he had an unusually attractive opportunity to buy the modest home he was living in, adding that he hadn't enough money to do so and hadn't sufficient credit at the bank. Mr. Mott accompanied the young man to his home, figured that the price was very reasonable, and arranged to enable the young man to finance the purchase of it, telling him he could repay the amount at his convenience.

How do I know this? Harry Bassett told me. He ought to be a good authority, since he was the young man.

Unlike too many of our financially successful business men, Mr. Mott has cultivated many of the finer things of life. He can appreciate good pictures and has personally collected quite a number of fine ones. He is musical. His home contains many beautiful art objects. He is widely read.

The Mott farm is operated on scientific lines. Mr. Mott breeds Holsteins and O. I. C. hogs; he raises the finest of white leghorns and Rhode Island reds, as well as geese and ducks; he keeps horses; he has won prizes with his cows.

And yet, with it all, he is never rushed, never apparently in a hurry, he is always cool, deliberate, self-possessed.

I forgot to tell how, when he was mayor of Flint, he would personally visit poor people who sent in complaints or tales of woe and that sometimes, when it was not within the province of the city to extend relief, Mr. Mott did so himself without saying a word to any one. Oftener than once on such visits he turned plumber to overcome an emergency.

It may still be that C. S. Mott will one day sit in the Governor's chair at Lansing.

B. C. F.

CHARLES W. NASH

UNLIKE most American youths, this farm-boy knew what he wanted. He wanted, first, to become a mechanic. He became a mechanic, master mechanic, so skilled a mechanic and so skilled in business that he rose to be a president.

Again he knew what he wanted. He wanted to establish an enterprise of his own. He knew exactly what kind of product he wanted to produce and he knew exactly the kind of men he wanted to draw around him. He hung out his shingle in the Summer of 1916.

In nine years he sold $418,761,674 worth of his product.

The profits reached $56,769,233.

Each single share of the original common stock had attained a market value of $2,250.

There were times when earnings far exceeded 100 per cent. in a year.

Before being split up, in 1925, the shares sold on the New York Stock Exchange far above those of any other concern in the industry.

The ex-farm-boy is not only one of the very largest income tax payers in the land, but has won a unique reputation for his managerial as well as mechanical ability. That, in brief, is the record of Charles W. Nash, motor manufacturer.

Says Mr. Nash: "There is only one sure recipe for success in any field of endeavor: Determination, close application to details, plus hard work and then more hard work.

"Years of experience have taught me that there are three highly important factors entering into the success of any large manufacturing organization, and these factors are machinery, methods, and men. And the last is, perhaps, the most important of all.

"It is obvious that no organization can become of higher caliber than the men who comprise it and direct its various activities. Therefore, when the Nash Motors Company was about to become a reality this problem of men was the most important I had to face. For I knew that, if I could surround myself with men of broad and successful experience, my success would be practically assured."

Experience has also taught Mr. Nash this: "Unproductive labor and waste are two things a manufacturer has to fight. It is not labor costs that cut into profits; it is the cost of unproductive labor — that and waste of material. These two things require constant attention."

You continually hear that the biggest problem in industry to-day is not production but selling. How has Mr. Nash achieved such success in selling his product that many times during the last few years orders have far exceeded productive capacity? Here is his answer, in eight words:

"Selling is 90 per cent. a production problem."

The plant designed by Nash embodied in a degree

CHARLES W. NASH

not excelled by even the Ford plant the principle of "straight-line" production; every material moved in a straight line from the point of delivery to the delivery of the finished product. Young Nash, at a very early age, mapped out a straight line course for himself. Born at DeKalb, Ill., on January 28, 1864, his family moved from their farm there to one near Flint, Michigan, when he was two. Although "bound out" on a farm at seven, he contrived to get a fair amount of schooling.

But as he had conceived a very definite vision of first becoming a mechanic and then setting up a business of his own, he began to qualify by supplementing his schooling by study at night. He had to exercise patience for several long, dragging years. They were, however, years of preparation and perseverance. He diligently studied things which he calculated would better equip him to form and run the manufacturing business of his dreams.

When twenty-eight he got a job as trimmer with the Flint Road Cart Company, later known as the Durant-Dort Carriage Company. His pay was a dollar a day. But his work quickly attracted the attention of J. Dallas Dort, and promotion followed promotion. The business was developed into the largest maker of horse-drawn vehicles in the world.

But it did not develop any more than young Nash developed. He became general manager and it was during his régime that the company enjoyed its most prosperous years.

The automobile, however, was making serious inroads on horse-drawn vehicles. Nash, always forward-looking, saw that he must make a bee-line for the motor manufacturing field.

The year 1910 harassed many companies and industries. Various automobile companies were hit. Bankers and boards of directors searched the country for the best managerial brains to rescue and rehabilitate their enterprises. Mr. Nash was the man picked to set the Buick Motor Company on its feet.

When he took up his duties as president and general manager, in 1910, he found an uncomfortably large inventory. Also, he discovered that the company was experiencing difficulty with a model which it had put on the market.

How did the new president meet the situation?

He developed a six-cylinder Buick — a six-cylinder, note. This car, combined with Nash's drastic reduction and subsequent rapid turnover of inventory, and his economical, skilful handling of the company's finances, proved the salvation of Buick. Within two years Nash had transformed a struggling concern into one of the foremost and most notably successful in the whole automobile industry.

This achievement, acknowledged and acclaimed throughout the automobile world, was rewarded by the elevation of Nash to the presidency and general managership of the General Motors Company, the parent organization, in 1912. This was recognized as the blue ribbon of the industry. Nash rose to the responsibility and further enhanced his reputation.

CHARLES W. NASH

But the straight line he had mapped out for himself did not end here. His aim and end was to organize a manufacturing business of his own. Notwithstanding the power and the financial reward which went with the presidency of the towering General Motors Company, he decided to strike out.

In July, 1916, he organized the Nash Motors Company and took over the Thomas B. Jeffrey Company of Kenosha, Wisconsin.

In 1919, he sold more than $40,000,000 worth of cars at a net profit of more than $5,000,000, and in the following year sales exceeded $57,000,000 and profits $7,000,000, these earnings representing more than $91 a share and $120 a share.

How did he do it?

He had clear-cut ideas and from the start applied all his exhaustless energy to carrying them out. First, he was determined to build a car embodying honest worth. He chose a price level which held out possibilities of a very wide market. Although four-cylinder cars were then the vogue among low-priced and medium-priced cars, Nash supplemented his four-cylinder line with a six-cylinder product.

He had originated a six-cylinder car to pull Buick out of its hole, and again he proved the merit of six cylinders. Even to this day Nash has refused to be carried away by the excursions of others into the field of multiple cylinders, although twelve cylinders were at one time hailed as the acme of perfection. He still pins his faith to six cylinders as standard.

To turn out the right product at the right price, Nash selected his associates with keen discernment. He announced that all through the works, wherever practicable, the men would be paid according to results. A minimum wage, guaranteeing the worker a living, was fixed, but as soon as the operative developed skill he was put on piece-work. Some 90 per cent. of Nash factory workers are on piece-work.

Somehow, Nash had evolved or assimilated very emphatic concepts concerning inventory and turnover. His record in this direction probably never has been matched.

It has not been unusual for Nash to turn over his stock of raw materials better than twelve times a year.

Says one of his factory lieutenants: "Just as rapid turnover of the goods on his shelves is sought by the retail merchant, so also is rapid turnover of stocks in his bins insisted upon by Mr. Nash. Long before the advent of the motor car, Mr. Nash grasped the value of a small inventory and quick turnover. This policy may have been mothered by necessity, but the fact remains that it has been one of the most potent factors in the outstanding success that has always attended the manufacturing plans of the president of Nash Motors.

"Ordinarily, Nash Motors never has on hand more than a full month's supply of materials. Certain items, of course, are bought well ahead, but others are scheduled so closely that they come in every week.

CHARLES W. NASH

As contracted with a plant where raw materials do not turn more often than once a year, there is a tremendous difference in the matter of floor space, interest charges and insurance, to say nothing of the hazard attendant upon the possibility of an abrupt change in business conditions."

Having come up through the ranks, Nash knew every minute operation entering into the making of a motor car. This knowledge he utilized to the full by spending a large part of his time moving from one end of the plant to the other. He scrutinized everything. Studiously eliminating waste motion, he rigidly checked the waste of material. He ceaselessly studied how to quicken the flow of production.

His theory was — and is — that raw materials on hand are a liability, rather than an asset, until they are fashioned into a finished product and turned into cash. Materials received at one end of the plant move forward after each operation in a straight line towards the center of the factory, here meeting in finished form those coming from the opposite end, body and chassis are assembled and, presto, the completed car rolls through the door.

Every brain in the plant, from foreman to president, meets every Monday afternoon at 5 o'clock to offer and hear suggestions for improving this process or that, to consider communications from owners and dealers offering comments or constructive criticism, to discuss conditions, sales plans, etc. Always when at home Mr. Nash presides over these sessions.

He pays particular attention to communications from the outside, for, as he frequently impresses upon his associates, "We don't pretend to know it all here at the factory." Also, he occasionally voices the reminder that, "The Nash product is the result of co-operation, extended by our partners in the business, the Nash dealers." He keeps the door to his office open always. Dealers, owners, the "boys in the factory," all are welcome to approach the boss.

Another factor has contributed to Nash's phenomenal success. His boyhood ambition, as already told, was to become a manufacturer. Nash, the man, was not content to become a mere assembler of motor parts manufactured by others. He became a manufacturer in the real sense of that word. Almost the entire car is fashioned, processed, produced in Nash's own plant.

As part of his preconceived program, Nash in 1919 acquired a half-interest in the Seaman Body Corporation of Milwaukee, builders of high-grade closed bodies, and he promptly proceeded to build a new manufacturing plant for this branch of his enterprise. In 1922 Nash Motors acquired control of the Lafayette Motors Corporation plant, adjacent to the Nash plant at Milwaukee, and in 1924 Mr. Nash organized the Ajax Motors Company, to take over the plant and property at Racine, Wisconsin, formerly belonging to the Mitchell Motors Company. The record of this new six-cylinder car will be watched with interest by the automobile world.

Even these acquisitions did not suffice to cope with

the call for the cars sponsored by C. W. Nash. Extensive expansions were instituted towards the end of 1924 and these have since added 30 per cent. to productive capacity. The Nash plants entered 1926 with capacity to produce 100,000 Nash cars.

Like other large-volume manufacturers, Mr. Nash has devoted serious thought to the increasing congestion in cities and on highways arising from the rapid multiplying of motor vehicles. Mr. Nash sees one interesting tendency; namely, a wider demand for medium and small cars and a diminishing demand for very large cars. Consequently, he has fortified his position to take advantage of this trend.

" I believe that automobile owners are doing their part to ameliorate congestion by the readiness with which they have accepted the medium-priced and moderate-sized car," declares Mr. Nash. " Practically all the makers who formerly produced only large cars are now making a smaller and lighter type.

" The public now recognizes that in these lighter and medium-priced cars it is getting a vehicle which, with proper attention, will give the maximum of service for five to seven years, and records show that only a small percentage of motor owners go as long as that before getting a new car.

" The traffic congestion problems are turning the attention of the motor public to the feasibility, if not the actual necessity, of the moderate-sized car for travel, not only in city streets, but in the country.

" I have studied this traffic congestion problem by

noting the types of cars in the endless stream of vehicles seen on all the main thoroughfares in the leading cities of our country, and I am firmly convinced that the traffic congestion problem is being relieved by the smaller wheel base car, as contrasted with the heavy and very long cars which were seen in a higher proportion half-a-dozen years ago than to-day.

"The great advantage of the smaller car is its easy handling and ability to turn in comparatively small space. I believe that the old type of extra luxurious, long wheel-base car will be virtually eliminated. The time is soon coming, I believe, when we will see on the roads scarcely any cars exceeding a chassis wheel base of 125 inches, and the majority of cars in use, I predict, will be 110 inches or less.

"There doubtless always will be a demand for a limited number of the larger cars, and the makers who have established a reputation for their product and maintain it will be able to keep their factories in production with very satisfactory returns. There will be a stable market for the big cars, as there is for the specially designed custom body, but compared with the 3,000,000 to 4,000,000 cars which may be made every year, the demand will be limited and supplied by a few makers."

What is to happen to the hundred and one concerns now turning out every conceivable variety of car?

"I feel," said Mr. Nash late in 1925, "that the automobile industry, like practically every other large industry, will ultimately gravitate to a few large or-

ganizations. I look upon the present as a testing-time which will lead to the passing of the weak and the survival of the fittest.

"It is significant that, in 1924, representatives from fifty-seven manufacturers took part in the drawing for space at the annual automobile show in New York and that the 1925 drawing fell to forty-seven. I look for a still smaller number in future.

"Prices in the industry have been fairly well stabilized and are not likely to show very drastic changes. The truth is that the motor car buyer to-day gets greater value for his dollar, compared with the cost of things in 1914, than the purchaser of any other class of merchandise. The automobile is actually cheaper now than it was ten years ago, notwithstanding the tremendous rise in wages and the increased cost of materials — wages are up 100 per cent. or more and materials anywhere from 50 to 100 per cent. Mass production, of course, has made this possible, combined with greater experience and skill in management.

"In one direction we can look for far-reaching developments. The motor bus is only in its infancy. Regulation has not yet been standardized by the various states or by different municipalities; but this will be straightened out in due course."

Mr. Nash early foresaw the potentialities of selling cars on credit instead of demanding total payment in spot cash, as was the custom originally. As one of Mr. Nash's chief associates, Vice-President W. H. Alford, expressed it:

"The automobile financing corporation made possible a vast increase in motor car buying. It opened up a new market, the great middle-class. The salaried man and the wage earners were able for the first time to enjoy the pleasures of owning an automobile. The credit plan has become the very heart and foundation of the motor car business. That it is absolutely sound in principle is evidenced by the fact that over 90 per cent. of all car owners in the United States to-day have taken advantage of it. That it is enabling millions to enjoy the happiness and benefits of automobile ownership is manifested by the still more impressive fact that of America's total car owners 80 per cent. — or more than three-fourths — have incomes of less than $2,000 a year.

"There is grave danger, however, if in attempting to expand this service, the initial payment is reduced and the financing period extended to a point that the security is weakened and re-possessions bring disaster to the financing companies."

The expansion — and the profits — of Nash Motors have been the talk, not only of the automobile industry, but also of investors in securities. Mr. Nash's axiom, " Selling is 90 per cent. a production problem," has needed revision. With Nash, selling for a long time has been 100 per cent. a production problem. Month after month all the cars that could be produced were sold before they left the factory floor.

The company makes no distinction between union and non-union employees. All are treated with equal consideration. The employees have formed a club or society, to which they contribute fifty cents a month. Twenty cents is used for social and athletic activities and thirty cents is placed in a fund for mutual aid in cases of sickness or misfortune. About 90 per cent. of the employees are members.

This club has its own orchestra, the company co-operates with it in maintaining a band, it has its own moving picture machines, and its own board of directors, composed of members.

On its part, the company maintains an athletic field, a tennis court, a club house and baseball field with a seating capacity of 6,000. The Nash Company boasts a semi-professional baseball team.

In addition to most modern hospital equipment and the like, the company manifests in a very practical way its interest in the happiness and well being of its people by making temporary loans when such assistance is helpful, by furnishing free legal advice, by examining property titles for employees contemplating buying a home, by lending money to home-builders, by making necessary financial arrangements for employees who desire to buy stock in the company, etc., etc.

Mr. Nash gets more fun and satisfaction from his association with "the boys" in the organization than from "society." He is an enthusiastic baseball fan, he likes to hunt big game, he is fond of fishing in the Northern woods of Michigan or Wisconsin, and he indulges in an occasional game of golf.

"But," says one who knows him intimately, "if you would watch this manufacturer of motor cars enjoying the recreation which he likes best, you would not have to travel any farther than his home in Kenosha and see him in action with his four little grandchildren. He is even a greater success as a granddaddy than as a motor manufacturer."

This same associate remarks, also: " Mr. Nash's office on the second floor of the administration building in Kenosha is typical of the man himself; it is well furnished but extremely modest; no rug adorns the floor, but the chairs are comfortable and the broad flat top desk at which Mr. Nash works cost less, perhaps, than the desk of many a chief clerk or office manager. And as any man in the Nash organization will testify, the door to that office is always open.

" The candor and friendliness of this strong, quiet man, who is efficient, progressive and yet unassuming in manner, accounts in large measure for the success he has attained since that day more than thirty years ago when he took his first factory job."

If you pressed Mr. Nash to sum up in one word the quality or characteristic or equipment more vital than all things else for the attainment of success, he would reply, " Commonsense."

A man who, in the short space of nine years, has built up a business on which there is not a dollar of bonded indebtedness, whose stocks have a market value approximating $137,000,000, whose profits have exceeded $56,000,000, and whose bank balance tops $30,000,000, surely must be regarded as a very practical authority on what makes for success.

B. C. F.

R. E. OLDS

THE town clock at Lansing, Michigan, was just pealing out three long strokes one Spring morning, in 1886, when young Ransom Olds crept softly out of his bed, slipped into his clothes, and made his way down to a little shop on River Street.

All night long he had tossed on his bed and had imagined himself riding down the street in the queer little car which he now examined critically. It was crude, built as it was from the various parts which he had been able to pay for out of his careful savings. The body was made of whitewood, the frame was substantially built of oak, and this somewhat ungainly superstructure rested on three steel-tired buggy wheels of conventional size.

What troubled him most was the transmission, for its construction was crude indeed. The rear axle had a ratchet on each side and it was steered by an iron lever. The main drive wheel was an iron wheel with half-inch pointed pins screwed into the face to make a sprocket. The driving chain, made of strap iron, with rollers on pins to hold the links together, was operated through a set of lathe gears — the transmission! Unfortunately there was no transmission case, and when the car was run the wood supports for the gears magnified the noise, like a sounding board.

When young Olds ran his motor vehicle out on the street in the early morning, the terrific noise of the gears shattered the peaceful silence and aroused the entire neighborhood. Within five minutes his progress had caused so much excitement that he decided a few hundred feet was sufficient for the first exhilarating tryout.

All this would have been embarrassing enough without the attending comment which punctuated every spasmodic jerk of the car.

But the boy was too much in earnest to let anything like that hamper his future progress. He had a big dream; it was to see the motor take the place of the horse.

Pliny Olds, his father, was one of the best mechanics in that section of the country, and from his earliest childhood the boy had spent his spare moments tinkering away in the little old lean-to beside the barn.

"That kid of yours will blow his head off some day, Pliny," the neighbors advised his father when the boy began building engines, but his father let him alone and nothing happened.

The Olds shop was a small building, with a lean-to at the back which contained an old boiler and an engine to furnish the motive power. "Ranny's" easy job as a growing boy was to rise at five o'clock every morning, build two fires at home, and then get up steam at the shop, so that there would be heat and power when his father and older brother came down. After this came breakfast and then school. At four o'clock he was back working in the machine shop or at odd outside jobs. Saturdays and vacations were spent at the shop, for which at first he received no pay.

After two years of this experience he was given fifty cents a day during Summer vacations.

When he had finished high school he was an expert machinist and good at pattern making and moulding. During all this period he saved every cent he could possibly put aside, and by the time he was twenty-one he was able to buy a half-interest in the shop, for which he paid $300 down and gave his father a note for $800, carrying 8 per cent. interest. This he paid off later.

"Engines were the one thing I could never get out of my head," said Mr. Olds. "At the time I went in with him, father's work consisted mostly of repairing, but I wanted to manufacture and it seemed to me that we could create a demand for small steam engines. We gradually worked out plans for a small engine and boiler of one or two horsepower, which could be operated by an ordinary stove burner. But there was so much deposit in the river water that the small boilers filled up with mud and were not very satisfactory. Next I invented a gasoline motor which was the first manufactured in the United States to use gasoline directly in the cylinder. We made this up as high as twelve to eighteen horse power."

These engines sold so well that the plant was enlarged and a factory was built, but the rapid expansion and some bad accounts soon threatened to swamp them. Borrowing all the money they could, the two men gave every ounce of their strength to getting the business on its feet.

"But in all that time I never lost faith in my idea of gasoline locomotion," Mr. Olds assured me. "All through those months I spent every spare minute tinkering with engines and experimenting with different forms of combustion. That little gasoline engine I had invented sold so well that it finally pulled us out of the hole and it convinced me more than ever that mechanical power as applied to all our regular functions was the coming solution of big business."

Working with all his might to build up the business on gasoline engines, Olds spent all his leisure time on his car. He worked in the shop during the day, gave his evenings to experimentation on his car, and then posted the books and attended to correspondence before he locked the doors at night.

Within three years the company found itself again on its feet. In 1890 it was incorporated as the Olds Gasoline Engine Works, Inc., with a capital of $30,000, and R. E. Olds was made president and general manager.

Before long the engines were being shipped from coast to coast, and quite an export trade was built up with Great Britain. In 1896 the Olds Motor Vehicle Company was organized, with a capital of $50,000, Olds having bought out his father four years before.

"It is funny how an idea sticks when you once get it into your head," Mr. Olds continued. "The gasoline engines were our bread-and-butter business, and most people thought the car was just a toy, but I knew that the car was my big venture.

"In 1891 I produced a steam horseless carriage with a flash boiler, which was much more quiet and more successful in every way. It became so talked about that the 'Scientific American' sent a man up to Lansing to look it over and published an article about it which aroused interest all over the world."

As a result of the publicity it obtained, Mr. Olds rather reluctantly sold his steam car for shipment to India.

"Just as soon as it left Lansing I set to work to adapt the internal combustion engine to the horseless carriage," he continued, "and this second car was completed in 1895, but not in time to compete in the Chicago 'Herald' contest. This second machine had high wheels and one and one-half inch rubber tires, but the engine formed the reach and was carried on the running gear."

A few years' use of the car thoroughly convinced Olds that he had a marketable proposition, and by this time the people in Lansing had begun to waken up to the fact that they had a remarkable new invention at their very door. In 1896, E. W. Sparrow, a local capitalist, became interested in the car and persuaded S. L. Smith, a former Lansing man, and Henry Russel, of Detroit, both men of means, to put some money into a company to put it on the market. At that time Lansing had a population of under 2,000 and there were no paved streets; so it was decided to locate the factory in a larger place, and Detroit was selected as the most desirable location.

The Olds Motor Works was incorporated in 1899, with a paid-in capital of $350,000. It absorbed the Olds Motor Vehicle Company and the Olds Gas Engine Works, and R. E. Olds was made president and general manager.

"It was our plan at that time," Mr. Olds informed me, "to put out a model which would sell for $1,250. I had fitted it up with some very up-to-the-minute improvements — pneumatic clutch, cushion tires, and electric push-button starter. We thought we had quite a car, but we soon found that it was too complicated for the public. That first year we ran behind about $80,000.

"The prospects of the industry were not very bright. Winton was making some cars down at Cleveland, Ohio, and Duryea, Haynes, and Apperson were all in the market. But the public persisted in the idea that it was not a practical proposition and would be a thing of the past within a year or two.

"You can't buck up against public opinion if it persists in a thing. You have to get around it some way; so I tried to size up the situation. Finally, after a long sleepless night, I decided to discard all my former plans and build a little one-cylinder runabout, for I was convinced that if success came it must be through a more simple machine.

"The plans which had formulated in my mind were very clear. It was my idea to build a machine which would weigh about 500 pounds and would sell for around $500. The result was the curved-dash "Oldsmobile," weighing 700 pounds and selling at $650. My whole idea in building it was to have the operation so simple that anyone could run it and the construction such that it could be repaired at any local shop. We rushed a few of them out as fast as possible, and they tested out so well I decided to put them on the market immediately.

"We sold 400 the first year, which was considered a wonderful achievement for that period. Having felt our way carefully, I decided that the only plan to recover from the slump we had had the first year would be to come out with an announcement that the following year we would build 4,000 machines. I thought this would restore confidence in the industry and I staked all I had on the success of my plan. It left me no other course than to make good, and the following year we not only produced but actually sold nearly the number planned.

"Past experience had taught me that the making of a car was one thing and the marketing another. Having planned my big production schedule for 1902, I knew it would take all the effort we could muster to sell those cars. To sell almost twice as many cars as there were in the country from one factory alone seemed like an impossible proposition, but we set to work.

"We got Roy D. Chapin, who was testing for us, to drive the car to the automobile show in New York

City, so that we could use the trip as an endurance test. It was. I guess Chapin would testify to that, to this day. As near as I can find out he had all the trouble that could possibly be created by one small car.

"*But he got there.*

"I was waiting for him at Madison Square Garden, and we used 'all there was in the shop' to put that car over. We finally got A. G. Spalding & Co. interested to the extent that they considered taking the New York agency and ordering 100 cars, but later discussion in a directors' meeting disclosed that they could not see the possibility of selling 100 cars in New York City; so they withdrew their proposition. This was a serious blow to us, but there is always a bright side.

"We had a man in Cleveland by the name of R. M. Owen, who had been doing some good work selling cars. Together with Roy Rainey, who was backing him, he attended the show. They were so enthusiastic about the car that Rainey offered to back Owen in opening up a New York agency, and they proposed making a contract to sell 500 cars. They were a game pair, and I knew they would make good, so I said, 'Why not make it a thousand cars, boys, and get some notice?' This they agreed to, and a contract was drawn that night.

"Rainey was a clever fellow who thoroughly understood the value of publicity. He and Owen started out by doing stunts with the cars on Fifth Avenue to attract attention. They got themselves arrested for speeding, upset a bicycle policeman, and made the car so talked about that people began to look into the matter seriously. That year 750 cars were sold in New York City, and the plant had to announce a waiting list."

But all did not go smoothly even then. Olds worked day and night to perfect his runabout. The first model had been completed and the blue-prints were all ready for production when a workman at the new factory pulled his forge fire too close to a large rubber bag filled with gas to supply an engine. A terrific explosion followed, and the fire spread so rapidly that those upstairs were barely able to save themselves. In an hour the entire factory was in ruins. Practically all the blue-prints of the old as well as the new model went up in the conflagration.

But right here interposed a peculiar twist of fortune. J. J. Brady, a young timekeeper at the plant, heard the first blast of the explosion, jumped from his stool and made a dash for the section of the factory where the new model was standing. Calling on those around for aid, he dragged and pushed the only model of the new car out into the open.

Just as soon as the little organization could be brought together again this car was taken to pieces, blue-prints were drawn, and the new car was built from a duplication of the parts. Olds was very ill in a hospital at the time, but within a month his men drove the new car under his window to assure him that all was well.

Arrangements were made to rebuild the same property but it was soon found that more extensive quarters were necessary. Lansing made overtures to Olds, and a plant was started there which grew to large proportions.

There is no question that the success of the Olds company stimulated Henry Ford, who was a frequent visitor at the Detroit plant from the very first. At that time Ford was working on a night shift as engineer for the Edison Company and was getting $1,000 a year. He would come over into the shops in the afternoons and watch them make the tests. Once one of the men asked him how much he was getting and Ford told him with some pride.

"If you're getting that in cash," said the man, "on a sure-fire job, you'd better cut out your interest in this proposition and stick to what you are at."

All this time other companies were coming into the field, and Olds, who was a born pioneer, not only encouraged them, but gave many of them mechanical aid. At that time he had about thirty patents which were infringed on with pathetic persistency, but he refused to take any action.

But there were breakers ahead for the Oldsmobile company. Olds's practical ideas for a popular low-priced car were not shared by some of the other executives of the company who were ambitious to put out a large and expensive car modeled along the lines of the foreign cars which were then being displayed at the auto shows. This was about January, 1904.

"We had done so well by that time," asserted Mr.

Olds, "that I thought I had about all I needed, and rather than hamper the ideas of the rest of the group I sold out my stock and decided to take a long vacation. But it did not work that way.

"While up in Northern Michigan with my family I received a wire asking me to return to Lansing. As I stepped off the train I was met by an old friend who handed me a very interesting looking paper. Reading it I found that a group of my friends had organized a half-million company of which I was to be the head, and within three hours had raised the money to finance it. Of this I was to have a controlling interest, or $260,000. To say that I was astounded would be putting it mildly. But I was still young enough to enjoy the harness.

"This happened in August, 1904, and we got to work so quickly that within a month ground was broken for the new factory, and by October 15 we ran out the first Reo car for trial. Of course it was built in temporary quarters. By November 20, I had personally driven this car over 2,000 miles in tests besides superintending the construction of the plant and its equipment, and had placed orders for the material for the first 1,000 Reo cars. And by the middle of March we shipped our first carload of cars. Before the end of the season we had shipped 300 carloads and sales had amounted to $1,378,000. The following year shipments reached 100 carloads a month, and we had more business than we could handle."

The fact that Mr. Olds's reputation is such that he

can practically choose his people where he will, accounts for a very interesting organization which has been gradually built up from employees of years' standing. Richard H. Scott, now president of the company, was in charge of Olds's gas engine plant up to the time of the organization of the Reo company, when he became its superintendent. D. E. Bates, secretary and treasurer, came to Mr. Olds from one of the banks, where his financial training had been such that he attracted the attention of Olds. H. T. Thomas, engineer, has been with him for twenty-two years and acted in the same capacity with Oldsmobile. When Olds left the Oldsmobile Company, Thomas took a position in the East, and one of the first acts of Olds the day after the new company was formed was to wire Thomas to come on and help him in designing the new Reo car.

"The automobile has brought more progress than any other article ever manufactured," says R. E. Olds. "It has not only carried the farmer to the city, but has given the city man a taste of the open. It has created and built up new markets, it has quickened trade and raised the standards of living, it has opened up new localities to greater production, and it has helped very materially to make America the headquarters of mass production."

O. D. F.

ALFRED P. SLOAN Jr.

THE man who holds the most important executive position in the automobile world, Alfred P. Sloan, Jr., president of General Motors Corporation, with its facilities for producing 1,300,000 high-grade cars a year and ramifications covering 144 countries, made these penetrating observations when subjected for the first time to the ordeal of answering questions about his life's experiences, about his recipe for handling men (the members of the General Motors family employ over 135,000 men), and about his vision of the future of the automobile industry:

" I never give orders.

" To attain the fullest measure of success for his company, an executive must ' sell ' himself, must sell his ideas to his associates.

" Perhaps an executive, through years of building up confidence, might get to the point where he could afford to say, ' You do this because I ask you to.' But an executive is wrong so many times himself that this would be a dangerous course to follow. He would miss so many opportunities for obtaining wise counsel. It is better to appeal to the intelligence of a man than to the military authority invested in you.

" The president of a company may have the right to fire any man out of the organization; but, if he is wise, he will ' sell ' the man rather than fire him.

"In our corporation arbitrary orders are not issued from the top. Even though we may start from many positions which seem to be different, we always thrash a thing out until we finally reach a point where we can agree.

"General Motors is a group organization. I have just returned from Detroit, where I consulted everybody who could possibly contribute to a certain decision which had to be reached.

"What is the hardest problem of all in handling other men?

"From my own experience and from the experiences of heads of other large corporations, I can tell you. It is this: You must grant a large measure of responsibility to the man placed in an important position. Such a man has, of course, unusual ability, unusual brains. But it is often hard to bring home to such a man in such a position that he does not know it all, and that he could profit by counselling with others. All of us have some weakness. But most human beings do not like to admit even to themselves that they have human weaknesses and limitations. Therefore, it is often extremely difficult to get a man in the frame of mind where he will gladly seek to gather from other people in the organization what would offset, what would remedy his own weakness. Yet this must be done in a large organization to bring about a maximum of efficiency and effectiveness.

"The human problem is far more delicate and difficult to handle than any production problem or distribution problem or engineering problem or financial problem.

"Psychology and personality constitute at least 50 per cent. of the material requisite for success as an executive. I have seen men with fine minds who failed to make their plans effective because they lacked understanding of how to work with people. In our business I should say that this psychological ability and personality mean 75 per cent. of the necessary equipment. The ability to get people to work together is of the greatest importance. If people can get each other's point of view, disagreement as to policies and courses of action are usually slight.

"To be able to get at what is the real question at issue is to go far toward its solution. My work brings me in contact with men of diametrically opposite opinions, and yet I find that often the differences of opinion are due to differences in their conception of what is the vital point; one man argues pro and another argues con, and all the time they are talking about different things. I have seen meetings where men, all important leaders, have discussed for an hour without coming any nearer a solution, until some one had the psychological insight to isolate and clarify the real issue. Then agreement was reached almost at once.

"Yes. What one can do is limited by what one can sell, by one's ability to convince others what is necessary to be done.

"In most big organizations there are, just as there

have been in General Motors, certain products turned out which are excellent and some which are only fair. Every General Motors product is going to be better than the best is now. This can and will be brought about by concentrating the brainiest men, those who have produced the excellent products, upon improving the products which most need improving. To accomplish this, those in charge must first be brought into a receptive frame of mind. They must be 'sold' on the advisability and importance of supplementing their own knowledge and ability by accepting the best counsel others can bring to their assistance.

"In modern, large-scale industry there are two major forms of organization: centralized and decentralized.

"If General Motors was to be centralized, we would have one man in supreme charge of all sales, another in supreme charge of engineering, another in supreme charge of manufacturing, and so forth.

"We are organized on a decentralized plan. Each operation, like Buick, Cadillac, Chevrolet, Oakland or Olds car or G. M. C. Truck, is headed by the best man we can find for that job, and he is charged with full responsibility for the success of that entire organization. In this way we develop greater initiative, greater enthusiasm and a greater sense of responsibility.

"Talking of initiative, there is more room in the automotive industry than in most other industries — steel, for example — for originality. To the consumer of steel it doesn't make much difference who makes it.

ALFRED P. SLOAN, JR.

The automobile buyer, however, takes a different attitude. There is always a keen demand for originality.

"Looking ahead, and trying to analyze the future of the automobile industry, I can see —"

But before we take up the future, it will be in order to deal with the past, and particularly with the achievements of Mr. Sloan which caused Pierre S. duPont, in announcing the selection of Mr. Sloan as his successor in the presidency of the corporation, to say publicly:

"The greater part of the successful development of the corporation's operations and the building up of a strong manufacturing and sales organization is due to Mr. Sloan. I greatly admire Mr. Sloan and his business methods and look upon him as one of the most able partners in the management of General Motors Corporation and their interests."

Although born (in New Haven) as late as May 23, 1875, Alfred P. Sloan, Jr., has been connected with the automotive transportation business longer than most leaders. When quite a young boy he made up his mind to become an engineer, a fortunate circumstance in the light of subsequent events, for, without engineering training, Mr. Sloan would not be able to analyze every important mechanical problem with the skill he does in his present position.

About the time he was graduated as a Bachelor of Science from the Massachusetts Institute of Technology (in 1895) his father was induced to become associated, among his other interests, with the Hyatt Roller Bearing Company of Newark, N. J., then about ready to expire. Young Alfred was installed as a draughtsman. The gross business done during his first month with the company was under $2,000. The young engineer promptly took hold of operations and within six months profits were being earned. From then on not a single year ended in red ink. Under the presidency of young Sloan the business passed the $20,000,000 mark a year, with net reaching as high as $4,000,000.

"A technical man usually feels as if he had been suddenly thrown overboard when he takes charge of a concern and finds himself confronted with problems of financing. I early had to wrestle with financial problems, which, though they seem small when I look back, seemed and were big enough at the time," Mr. Sloan recalls.

In the building up of Hyatt Roller Bearing from a small, struggling, unprofitable venture to the biggest and most profitable of its kind in the world, Mr. Sloan gathered more than financial experience. He had to go out and hustle for orders.

Young Sloan had a part in the very birth of the automobile industry. His bearings were sought by the original pioneers in the new kind of transportation. Both the Haynes-Apperson and the Olds cars first took the road with Hyatt bearings. Henry Ford likewise chose Sloan's product when he entered the field. So did other adventurers into the arena, just as many leading automobile manufacturers have done ever since.

ALFRED P. SLOAN, JR.

His activities thus brought Sloan into direct contact with automobile leaders from the very start. In those days buying of supplies was not delegated to a subordinate, but was looked after by the principals themselves. The result was that Sloan built up as wide an acquaintanceship as any man ever identified with the industry, a circumstance which was to prove most helpful to him in his larger responsibilities.

One of Mr. Sloan's customers was W. C. Durant. On re-entering the industry after having temporarily lost control of his companies, Durant conceived the idea of acquiring a number of accessory companies, mainly to insure sources of supply for his General Motors. He particularly desired to include the Hyatt Roller Bearing Company and to have Mr. Sloan become head of the new combination. This was done, in 1916, Mr. Sloan becoming president of the United Motors Corporation, the name given the accessory group.

When United Motors was absorbed, at the end of 1918, by General Motors, Mr. Sloan became vice-president in charge of the half-score accessory companies, and was also made a member of the executive committee.

When Mr. Durant dropped out of General Motors for the second time, in December, 1920, things naturally were for a time in a state of flux. Shake a barrel of potatoes, and the big ones will come to the top. So was it with General Motors. It was not very long before Alfred P. Sloan was placed in charge of operations, with the title of operating vice-president, Pierre S. duPont having succeeded Durant as president. Within a year Mr. Sloan's aptitude for finance was recognized by his election as a member of the Finance Committee, the members of which included several of the ablest bankers in New York, namely, George F. Baker, Jr., of the First National Bank, Seward Prosser of the Bankers Trust Co., and E. R. Stettinius of J. P. Morgan & Co.

It gradually became taken for granted, both inside and outside the General Motors Corporation, that when Mr. duPont would retire from the presidency, which he had accepted temporarily as an emergency measure when he and his family and banking associates took over control, only one man would be considered as his successor, so thoroughly had Mr. Sloan demonstrated his all-round fitness for the chief-executiveship of the huge enterprise. Therefore, the publication of the following announcement by Mr. duPont on May 10, 1923, excited no astonishment:

" At the time of my election to the presidency of General Motors Corporation in December, 1920, it was understood that my term of office would be limited as to duration, and, further, that many of the duties of the president would fall upon the shoulders of the vice-presidents of the Corporation.

" Pursuant to this understanding, Mr. Sloan has assumed the responsibility of directing the operations of the Corporation under the general policies laid down by the Executive Committee. The greater part of the successful development of the Corporation's operations and the building up of a strong manufacturing and sales organization is due to Mr. Sloan. His elevation to the presidency is a natural and well merited recognition of his untiring and able efforts and successful achievements.

"I bespeak for Mr. Sloan a continuation of the loyal and active support that has been accorded him already by the officers and employees of the Corporation, its distributors, dealers and customers. I greatly admire Mr. Sloan and his business methods and look upon him as one of the most able partners in the management of General Motors Corporation and their interests."

Mr. duPont remained chairman of the board. A few days later Mr. Sloan was elected a director of the duPont Company. He also joined the board of the Chase National Bank.

When I wired one of Mr. Sloan's oldest and closest friends and associates, C. S. Mott of Flint and Detroit, to specify some of the qualities which had won Mr. Sloan such signal promotion, he immediately telegraphed this illuminating reply:

"Alfred Sloan is an indomitable worker; a systematic and persistent organizer; a stickler for procedure; a crystallizer of corporation policies for the benefit and protection of the customer, the stockholder and the members of the General Motors organization. His many years of training and experience in shop work, followed by taking over sales and executive duties, combined with natural ability and an open mind, make him an ideal man to direct the affairs of General Motors Corporation. Sloan and I have been warm personal friends ever since we started doing business together over twenty years ago. The satisfaction derived from my personal relations with him could not have been greater if he had been my own brother. I think he inspires the same confidence in all with whom he comes in close contact."

Please note these three words: *an open mind*.

All Mr. Sloan's associates agree that he has mastered every branch of the automobile industry, that he delves deeply into every engineering problem before passing judgment, that as salesman he graduated from the School of Hard Knocks, that he has wrestled successfully with expanding production all his life, that he can analyze financial questions with all the acumen of an experienced banker.

Yet, though he knows much, he does not feel that he knows it all, and it is this trait in him, this eagerness to seek counsel of others, this democratic open mindedness, which has won him the esteem and the ardent cooperation of every member of the General Motors family.

This phase of Mr. Sloan's character can be read in his countenance. He has not a hard, domineering mien. He radiates earnestness, but not severity. He talks in a moderate tone, and is totally without swashbucklerism.

Although Mr. Sloan long since passed beyond the need for working to accumulate more millions, he de-

ALFRED P. SLOAN, JR.

votes practically all his waking hours and every day of the year to his work. No sport is his hobby. Work is. A European trip, for example, does not mean in his case the rest it is supposed to be. General Motors has establishments dotting every part of the atlas, and the time other tourists devote to visiting cathedrals and art galleries or gambling tables, Mr. Sloan devotes to visiting his company's branches and agencies and offices.

As with Edsel Ford, his home and his wife are his only non-business interests. True, he has a phenomenally large number of friends, but all have been made in course of his life's work.

Even to-day he spends half of his time away from his office in New York, visiting plant after plant, digging into problem after problem, holding conference after conference with executives in factories and men on the firing lines. Men, materials, machinery, money, all receive his diligent attention — especially men, for Mr. Sloan holds that a proper understanding of human nature is necessary for the highest success in any line of business.

That, briefly, is the type of self-developed president guiding the destinies of one of the greatest organizations in the world, furnishing all grades of automobiles, from the low-priced Chevrolet to the coveted Cadillac in the higher-priced field.

Is it altogether astonishing that in the first year Mr. Sloan became president, the corporation nearly doubled its manufacturing capacity, entirely out of current earnings, and sold a record-breaking number of cars?

What of the future of the automobile industry? Under questioning, this was elicited from Mr. Sloan:

"Looking ahead and trying to analyze the future of the automobile industry, I can see no reason why our industry should not follow the trend followed in most other large-scale industries, such as steel, woolen, brass, copper, packing, harvesting machinery. We can expect to see in the next few years, first, the elimination of many companies, for the basic reason that, from an economic standpoint, they have no right to exist — sentiment does not enter into the operation of economic law. This will bring about a limited number of large institutions.

"Second, there doubtless will come consolidation of some of these into groups. These groups will each manufacture a complete line of cars, from low-priced to high-priced, where quantity production justifies such a policy."

I asked "When will this all come about?"

"It is dangerous to attempt to be a prophet," replied Mr. Sloan, smiling. "The time it will take will depend on how competitive the industry becomes. Economic necessity will bring about this evolution.

"There is every reason why an institution like General Motors, if properly managed, should attain and maintain a powerful place in the automotive field. For some years to come — how many, no one can foretell — those concerns having the brains capable of originating the best new ideas will enjoy a tremendous advantage. The automobile industry, it would hardly be an exaggeration to say, is still in its experimental stages. Many things which now enter our daily life, and which we now take as a matter of course, started as pure theories and those who propounded them usually were derided as being 'nuts.' So has it been in the automobile industry, and so it will continue to be.

"But General Motors is so constituted that it should be able to reduce the time required to take hold of new ideas and theories and put them into practicable application. We have an extraordinarily fine research department, under Mr. Kettering, who has the most wonderful analytical mind of any man I ever met and who combines with this faculty unlimited vision and courage.

"Under the generous inducements of our Managers Securities Company plan, providing for liberal profit-sharing with those who carry on the actual management of the business, we are in a position to hold and, whenever necessary, to reach out for the brainiest men in the whole industry. The future of any executive who becomes associated with our corporation and renders satisfactory service is abundantly assured. The advantages derivable from having employees become stockholders are almost beyond computation."

We next discussed the question of mortality among automobile dealers. Indicating that the coming evolution in the industry would tend to bring about more satisfactory conditions in this direction, Mr. Sloan emphasized how vitally important it is for a dealer to have or acquire the franchise of a responsible institution well financed and having a good product. The strength of the institution constantly becomes a matter of increasing consideration from the dealer's standpoint. Everybody in the industry realizes that a great many dealers are to-day representing institutions which will not be in existence some years hence. They are thus situated very insecurely.

The farsighted dealer of to-day seeks to represent an organization that is certain to expand when the industry expands and one that will take care of its dealers in times of lessened business activity, an organization able financially to stand back of the product and, if anything goes wrong — and things inevitably do go wrong once in a while — to carry on until things right themselves. Now that the automobile business is conducted on a very large scale, these conditions cannot be overlooked by the forehanded dealer.

"General Motors Corporation," added Mr. Sloan, "fully recognizes that the dealer is a most important link in the chain that completes any transaction. The dealer is entitled to a profit, but the consumer is entitled to have the dealer operate his business on a sound and economic basis so that the overhead is just. The dealer has capital at stake; so has the manufacturer. They should work more closely together than they have heretofore. There must be a closer liaison and better understanding than there have been in the past.

"The fault has not been entirely with the dealer; far from it. There are, however, still a good many economic features of the situation which have not yet fully asserted themselves, but which dealers possessing keen business intelligence will not fail to take into account in shaping their course."

President Sloan concluded our talk with these words, uttered in a tone ringing with confidence: "I thoroughly believe that in General Motors Corporation we have a complete institution, an institution embodying all the possibilities of tremendous development and increased effectiveness and efficiency. We have within ourselves the power, the brains, the resources, the experience to do tremendously bigger things than ever before. We have successfully overcome many problems which confronted the new management. We have been able to co-ordinate our efforts and operations. We have been able to instill the right spirit all through the organization, the spirit of loyalty and teamwork.

"We face the future with faith, without fear. We are capable of playing a worthy part in the development of this most important of all our newer industries."

As Mr. Sloan uttered these words, my mind flashed to the Admiral's laconic declaration that he and his fleet were "ready for a fight or a frolic."

B. C. F.

H. H. TIMKEN

BACK in the late eighties a man watched a train round a curve on a stretch of track not far from St. Louis. The rails were roughly laid and as the cars came bumping along over the uneven roadbed and hit the curve they rocked until the bumpers gritted against each other with a squeaking noise which could be heard for blocks.

As he stood there Timken's highly developed sense of efficiency suffered a shock.

Even under the most favorable conditions the bumpers ground against each other continuously. The rasping noise was bad enough in itself, but the conditions it indicated were even worse, for he well knew that under the stress of the rough roadbed and the uneven track the cars were subjected to sudden shifts which gave such a grinding thrust load to the axles that the wear and tear was enormous.

"That's a tough job to lick," he said with conviction to the man at his side, "but I think it can be done."

How it was done and the various stages of its development take one back to a little blacksmith's shop in St. Louis, Missouri, where a master mechanic with a vision as remarkable as his mechanical skill foresaw the enormous contribution which could be made to industry by the reduction of friction.

At the time this story opens H. H. Timken was hard at work in his father's shops, where Henry Timken, senior, was trying to perfect a more satisfactory anti-friction bearing. For years the senior Timken had toiled to eliminate the useless labor made necessary by dry and sticking wheels.

"One of the first things my father impressed on me in those early days," he said, "was that the man who could devise something which would reduce friction fundamentally would achieve something of real value to the world. Neither the ball bearings nor the straight roller bearings seemed to solve the problem completely, although they were of enormous help. What we were searching for was something which would reduce the tremendous wear which came because of their incapacity for thrust loads or adjustment for that wear. It was a comparatively simple matter to provide for the carrying of the radial load, which is up and down and which consists of the weight of the object and its load; the difficulty lay in providing for the impact of the end thrust, which consists of a load or shock coming from the side or the end. This is the force you feel when you are thrown to one side of an automobile when you are rounding a curve.

"Wherever there is resistance to motion we not only have serious mechanical strain but waste effort, whether the power is produced by human strength, by that of the horse, or by artificial means, and the producer pays not only for the wear and tear on his equipment but also for fatigue and lost effort. This covers not merely maintenance and actual loss of power, but also includes increased overhead and a lowered efficiency of man or machine.

"Matters of this sort were not so closely studied in the early days because quantity production was almost a thing unknown, but even then we knew that to be successful a bearing must not only aid the flow of motion, but that it must offer longer life, freedom from trouble, and less frequent lubrication than anything yet devised. Power and maintenance are two of the big costs of operation, and the greater the resistance the more power necessary to operate.

"One of the great questions of modern times is the increase of individual efficiency. Not only greater unit production as applied to individuals, but to the utilization of each mechanical unit to its maximum capacity. For instance, many of the big plants run their expensive machinery for twenty-four hours to lessen interest charges against the equipment.

"In the most efficiently run of our big plants men are being relieved of all unnecessary physical labor in order that they may conserve their strength and energy and direct it toward increased output. The high cost of pushage has always been an important factor in keeping up costs. Anything which will lower it contributes materially to industrial progress."

Back in the little blacksmith's shop and later on in his carriage shop in St. Louis the senior Timken had foreseen all these things with almost uncanny vision. As the little shop expanded into a four-story building of majestic proportions and his business increased, he continued to experiment in an effort to produce a bearing which would meet at the same time with equal resistance both the radial and the thrust loads. He finally found it in the tapered bearing.

Up to the time this bearing was perfected, in 1898, the senior Timken had built up a flourishing plant for the manufacture of carriages. He had been experimenting with bearings for many years and had equipped his carriage axles with roller bearings, making his vehicles unique. The venture had been so successful that a space 20 by 35 feet had been set aside on the crating floor and here five or six men were kept busy assembling the roller bearing axles. It was in this little spot that the first tapered bearing was made, and within this tiny area was founded the nucleus of the two great plants which now cover many acres in Canton and Columbus, Ohio, and three smaller plants at Walkerville, Ontario, Canada; Birmingham, England; and Paris, France.

Approximately 90 per cent. of all automotive vehicle manufacturers now use Timken tapered roller bearings; in fact, the Timken company produces a large percentage of all the bearings used in the United States.

The growth of the business may be best understood by a line of simple statistics. In 1902, 120,900 bearings were shipped, whereas by 1923 the volume had grown to 22,550,430, a monthly average of 1,900,000.

By the time the tapered bearing had come into being, both sons had become interested in the business, although their careers were in no way influenced by their father.

"To be successful you must be independent," was part of the advice he gave them. "If you want to lead in any line you must bring to it independence of thought, unfailing industry, aggression, and indomitable purpose. If you have an idea which you think is right, push it to a finish. Don't let anyone else influence you against it. If we all thought the same way there would be no progress. But above all don't set your name to anything you will ever have cause to be ashamed of."

"Nothing ever stuck in my mind like that," his son said as he talked with me. "If there was any one thing which fixed it in my mind that we must continue to make our product better and better it was the thought that it carried the family name."

True to his expressed conviction that the boys should map out their own careers, they were sent to college and allowed to choose their own training. H. H. Timken chose to study law. Always a keen analyst, the weighing of facts and the careful balance of justice intrigued him far beyond the ordinary routine of manufacture as he knew it at the time. He was graduated from law school with honor and was admitted to the bar, but later association drew him inexorably toward the lines along which his father was working.

A long European trip, during which he studied in considerable detail the progress being made by foreign inventors toward anti-friction bearings, finally cemented his decision. At that time the foreign field led us in experimentation along these lines, and the lad was a little piqued to think that we were not forging to the front. He determined to throw all the weight of his endeavor toward perfecting a bearing which would be superior to anything on the market.

"It did not take me long to find out that a desire to do anything is not worth the flip of a coin if it is not backed up by iron effort," Timken asserted as he dwelt on those days. "To get anywhere, a man must first see his goal, then lay his plans to attain it, and be prepared to buck up stiffly against every obstruction which threatens his way, beating them back until he conquers them.

"One thing which I learned later by experience was that no man can honestly and effectually run two or three different kinds of businesses which are not allied. To be proficient you must study your own business from the ground up, and you cannot do it when your mind is split up with a variety of interests. Men often get too thinly spread on the map and then blow up. A business must be strongly entrenched to stand adversity and the strain of bad weather, and its leader must keep his mind continually centered on his own particular line. In my opinion you can always do your work better by *sticking to one job.*"

When young Timken returned from abroad he settled down with his father and brother and began to study the requirements of the wagon industry. He began to visualize the relation a properly constructed bearing would have to the transmission of power, and he spent all his spare time analyzing the demands of modern machinery for better friction reducing methods. More and more he decided that they were on the right track for big results.

"Although I set aside law for production," he replied when I asked him about giving up his profession, "I have never regretted my legal training. It has helped me in every phase of my business. Without prejudice I can honestly say that I think a legal education is of value to every man who intends to enter large business. It teaches him to think straight, to plan wisely, to see the adverse side, and realize the obstacles he is going to meet. It makes him quick on the trigger, for he is trained to aggressive action, and it teaches him to look out for pitfalls.

"I am much in favor of young blood in a business," he continued. "We need young men to bring us new ideas and we should encourage them to try them out and give them a chance to make good. That is progress. But I believe in giving them a little opposition so that they will have a chance to show their initiative. The man who has to fight to maintain his ideas is the strong comer in the business game.

"Young men should train themselves to be more aggressive and more independent in thought. What we need in the business world is the quick wit to think our way out of a difficult situation, the independence of mind to see a new track, the courage to make a quick decision even if it does not coincide

H. H. TIMKEN

with the general opinion, and the backbone to put it over when we know we are right.

"One of the earliest things my father taught us was to look into the future and try to foresee events. As a growing boy I learned some very important lessons from his clear-sighted vision, for he had a remarkable sense of foresight along mechanical lines. From the first introduction of the automobile he predicted its success. Not only did he see it as a popular form of transportation, but he also sensed its unlimited possibilities for haulage. And he bent all his efforts toward devising a bearing which would be his contribution to that phase of progress.

"Our first experiments were with the cup-and-cone ball bearings and annular ball bearings. At that time alloy steels were comparatively undeveloped and the bearings did not stand up well under the tests. We worked along to get better alloys and then turned our attention to the tapered roller bearings which we tried out first on carriages and then on trucks. At that time my brother and I had taken over the active management of my father's wholesale carriage business in St. Louis, and when we found out how well the bearings were working out on our carriages and trucks, we began to think that the bearing business offered better possibilities than the manufacture of carriages; in other words, that the 'tail was beginning to wag the dog.' Therefore, we decided to get out of carriage manufacture and start making bearings.

"It was a vital decision and we had plenty of reason later on to wonder whether we were right, but we stuck to our idea that there was a great future for anything which would reduce friction. We have always kept as our vision, 'Less friction and longer life.'

"Like all other pioneers we had plenty of discouragements, but the worst difficulty we had was to obtain good steel. We soon found that the goal was fine steel, and how to get it was a serious problem. At that time each manufacturer was developing his own; there was no standard and no special effort to attain a standard.

"One of the most important problems in manufacturing bearings is that they shall be uniform. Any one can make a good thing once; the point is to keep it up to grade. Uniformity in mass production day in and day out means quality. To obtain this uniformity we found it advisable to make our own electric steel billets and tubing. We soon found that it made it possible to manufacture exactly the right analysis steel at a much lower cost than we could buy it from the outside — this of course meant a saving in bearing cost to our customers.

"A serious early trouble which developed was our inability to make the axles and bearings in St. Louis because of inadequate facilities. It was decided to move nearer to the steel market, and Canton, Ohio, was selected as a logical place where we could be nearer both to raw material and to our market, and where we would have room for expansion."

H. H. TIMKEN

By this time, 1903, the automobile business was beginning to develop rapidly. Many automobile manufacturers who used the bearings were putting them on both front and rear wheels, and were experiencing considerable difficulty in securing satisfactory axles. This offered the Timkens a wonderful opportunity of which they were not slow to take advantage. A complete line of front and rear commercial and passenger car axles were immediately designed for the trade, in which were installed the tapered roller bearings; and the bearings were not only introduced in the wheels but also in differentials, pinions and steering pivots, and transmissions. This entrée was memorable, for it marked a big step forward in the expansion of the company.

"All this sounds very easy," said Mr. Timken as we chatted together, "but we just about sweated our souls out down at the plant. We almost went broke several times, but we kept our credit good and were able to borrow money as we needed it. When we started in here at Canton, we did not have more than thirty or forty men. My brother looked after the sales and I followed up production. A good part of my time was spent working out and testing steel.

"Whenever I could get away from the plant I was out looking for business. *We did not expect it to come to us.* We visualized a big future for ourselves at the hands of the automobile manufacturers, and we were hot on the trail of every new inventor of a car. I used to spend days in Detroit and other cities hunting around back alleys and visiting the little machine shops to locate someone who was designing a car, so that we could persuade him to equip it with Timken axles. When we got hold of him we did not let up until we had persuaded him that the future success of his car lay in his adoption of our particular equipment. We worked with most of the big car manufacturers while they were still experimenting in their little machine shops. Olds, Winton, Packard, Haynes, Apperson — all were early customers of ours long before they were dignified by the name of manufacturers. We could get to a man who was building a few cars and often would find him experimenting with foreign ball bearing equipment. Then it was up to us to convince him that we could give him something of far greater bearing capacity and to persuade him to try it out for himself."

But no company ever forges to the front without serious setbacks. Early in the game one of the larger manufacturers asked the Timkens to figure on supplying complete front and rear axles. They put in their bid and got the order. When it came to figuring it over it was found that they had left out the cost of the wheels in making their calculation, and that to fill it would involve a serious loss. But the Timkens were game and stuck to their bargain. It won them not only future orders but also the respect of the industry.

Although his connection with the growth of the automobile industry is a particularly picturesque part of the progress of Timken's business, the installation of his bearings in other lines is of equal importance. Timken engineers work constantly in close connection with every form of development where industrial machinery is used. Cranes, elevators, conveyors, line shaft hangers, pillow blocks, logging blocks, drills, locomotives, mine cars and electric motors, and, in fact, practically all machinery comes within the province of anti-friction bearings.

Of interest in this connection is a break-down test made by Timken with a Timken-equipped electric motor. At the time this was written the motor had run 702,000,000 revolutions, and in that period the bearings were lubricated but twice; ordinarily the plain bearing motor requires lubrication weekly. To visualize 702,000,000 revolutions, comparison can be made with the 40,000,000 revolutions made by the bearings in the wheels of the average automobile over its entire seven years of operation.

By striving always to contribute to the growth of other industries, Timken bearings have played their part in making this country the home of quantity production. Mr. Timken says it is a modest part. "I am just a parts maker," he said to me quietly. "Don't rank me with the manufacturers."

Timken is absolutely a square shooter. Anything which bears his name must be the best that can be made. His ethics are high and his fetish is precision.

He loves horses, racing, fishing, hunting, speed boats, flying and all kinds of sport. Anything which is life and offers action appeals to him.

He believes in a certain autocracy of leadership, feeling that one man must stand unalterably in command at the helm, but he has never had a strike in his organization.

"We do not play politics here," he said. "This is an anti-friction organization."

O. D. F.

WALTER C. WHITE

ABOUT half a century ago, before Cleveland had written itself into history, a sturdy New Englander brought his little family from the East and bought a home just outside the city. Soon after, he organized the White Manufacturing Company which made sewing machines, and later entered the transportation field with bicycles and roller skates.

Thomas H. White was a man of remarkable character. His ideas were concise and definite. He believed that we do not get anything rightly in this world unless we work for it. He had an intense love of home, felt a deep responsibility in the careful upbringing of his children, and left no stone unturned to aid them in self-development.

He taught them to work things out for themselves. He did it after this fashion:

One day Walter C. White, then a boy of seven or eight, watched his older brothers sailing their boats in a big pond. He was consumed with an overwhelming desire for a boat of his own, and his boat was to be the pathfinder for all the others.

"Dad," he said eagerly that night, "had you thought of buying me a boat?"

Somewhat surprised, his father answered in the negative.

"Very well," said the boy; "then I will build one for myself."

"In that case," said his father, "I will furnish you with a good set of tools."

Later on he built an engine, getting his instructions from a book. But to his great disappointment, although the engine ran, it did not accomplish anything, for it had no pulling power. This taught him a lesson. A thing might move, but it was useless if it did not actively perform some definite function.

All this time he was learning other lessons as well. The youngest of seven, four of them boys, he got plenty of intensive training. The Whites lived in what was then the outskirts of the city. They had a large place, and the children were allowed to keep any animals that they would care for properly. Two pretty fast horses were at the boys' disposal if they drove them carefully. Otherwise they were forbidden.

"If I let you have a horse and you do not take care of him," said their father, "you cannot have him again. If you want the confidence of people you must not betray it."

In this way he built up a strong spirit of dependability and self-reliance. He trusted them implicitly, and they never betrayed his trust. In guiding their conduct he stuck to main principles and let them work out their own details. He did little talking, but he built these principles into his children with their growth and unconsciously they influenced all their actions. Sundays they all spent together and after dinner they had interesting discussions of current events. The senior White's views on all questions were sound and logical. They became a great influence to his children. Nevertheless all development was individual; he never forced them.

Once when Walter White was so small he could hardly tote a gun he asked permission to go shooting with his father. The senior White smiled, picked out the gun with the least " kick," and took the lad along. The first time young Walter pulled the trigger he was scared to death, and the recoil nearly knocked the breath out of him. The next time was better. In that way he learned to shoot. It was part of a liberal all-round education.

Walter White is fond of hunting. He rides to hounds, is a polo player and keeps a stable of a dozen polo ponies at his beautiful estate at Gates Mill. He is a breeder of fine cattle, is interested in everything that savors of sports, and is one of the best horsemen in that part of the country.

When the time came for Walter to think about college his natural thought was to take an engineering course. He had a flair for mechanics, and mechanical engineering seemed to be his logical bent.

"If you take mechanical engineering," said one of his brothers who was a Cornell graduate, "you will get lots of shop work and you have already had that down at the plant. Take my advice and register for a general course so that you will get a broad outlook in all lines. Later on you can specialize."

"The advice sounded so good," said Walter White, "that it changed my entire plans. I took general science and got my B.S., but in the last two years I found myself with a growing desire to take up law. I took a law course and the Summer after my graduation I went down to father's factory as assistant to the assistant treasurer.

"Nobody will ever know how I hated the sight of that day book. The fact that I was keen about mathematics seemed to point to bookkeeping as my natural job, but I could not see that it got me anywhere. I wanted something which showed visible results. I was stagnating on the job, as misplaced as a frog in a bowl of goldfish."

Later, urged by a former classmate who had entered the New York Law School, he went to New York and read law with such vigor that he secured his degree in the Spring, planning to return in the Fall and take his examination for the bar.

That Summer he spent at home, and in the Fall entered the office of Judge Williamson, General Counsel for the New York Central, and a great friend of his father. The following Spring he was admitted to the bar.

"I had no false notions of my ability," he said. "That is always a great help. I stayed in Judge Williamson's office through the Summer and by Fall I knew I was on the wrong track again. I was a shark at mathematics, but I wanted problems I could work out. The law was not an exact enough science.

"But at the same time I felt I had had training

which was of the utmost value. I knew I had no ability as a lawyer, but on the other hand I did not seem to have a flair for anything. I think I felt a little discouraged with myself. Now I know that I was merely in that transitory period which comes to most boys and often to older men, when they do not know just exactly what they are fitted for. I had not as yet slipped into the right groove.

"About this time my brother was working hard on an automobile proposition. He had developed a steam boiler which was showing up pretty well. Father seemed to have a lot of confidence in it, and that decided me. I came home and went into the shop. First I tested, then I began producing engines. By that time I felt like a Jack-of-all-trades."

The question of patents was vital at this period. The Whites took out some fundamental patents and tried to get others from Germany, but the report was that they would not work. Their London attorney suggested that they send someone over to London to sell the White patents and demonstrate that they had a working model. The plan was to sell them later in Germany.

Walter White was selected for this job. He took a letter of credit, a car, a lot of parts, and sailed for England. This was in 1901, and he was then twenty-five years old.

While on his way to the boat he met a friend of his college days in New York City who was much interested in his errand.

"You're going to be up against it, Walter," he said.

"I'll tell you what I'll do. George Marcus is going over on the same boat. I'll give you a letter of introduction to him and he will start you right. It is important that you should get in right at the start."

White met Marcus and on the trip they got pretty well acquainted. The two went to the Hotel Cecil and White put up his car in a nearby garage. Marcus stayed in London a month, and in that time he did much to interest his friends and English relatives in the new car. In those days any car was a matter of interest, and a steam car of American design shown by a likeable young fellow from a sister country had great pulling power.

It may be that White overdid the interest end. At any rate he did not sell any patents, nor cars either. He says he "did not even know how to talk in sales language." Master salesman that he is to-day, it seems difficult to believe. The patents were to be sold on a royalty arrangement, but he was unsuccessful in even interesting a prospect. Those were the days when autos broke down once or twice every quarter of a mile or so, and enthusiasm lagged.

He joined the Automobile Club, got in with some old Cornell fellows and showed his car around a little.

Finally one prospect came to him and said:

"Where can I get one of those cars?"

White answered "In America," and promptly wrote the home office.

Back came a sizzling letter, asking why he did not sell the man a car and try to make some of his expenses.

That wakened him up and he went to work. He saw that he could not build up a sales organization from a hotel; so he took chambers and opened a display room.

"The most conspicuous display in that room was my ignorance," said White with a laugh when he was telling me about it, "but finally I did begin to sell cars. People were very nice to me and everybody helped all they could."

White stayed in London for three years, until the car was pretty well known on the other side; then he left it in good hands and returned to this country in 1904. But he was now rich in experience. Among other valuable lessons he had learned the prestige given a car by taking part in contests, army maneuvers, and other public events. At that time England and the continent were far ahead of us in motor tests, and England, as always, was in the lead in sports. When he returned to America he began to take part in endurance contests. He also got into correspondence with army engineers about supplying cars for the army.

At the time army maneuvers were being held at Manassas, and there were few chauffeurs in the army. He secured an invitation to General Corbin's mess and invited him for a drive. His was the only auto in the camp. He drove General Corbin everywhere, and by the time he left, that section of the army was thoroughly sold on the car. This marked the first thought of the introduction of the motor lorry.

Meanwhile, Windsor White was handling the administrative end of the business and Rollin White, who had exceptional mechanical designing ability, was running the factory. With such able management at the plant, Walter, as younger brother, was left free to promote interest in the car.

All this time the little company had been working along under the direction of the White Sewing Machine Company. The White Motor Company was occupying a small plant just outside the factory and the business was being developed entirely on sewing machine capital.

In the Fall of 1901 the output of cars was three a week. By 1906 the business had grown to 1,500 cars a year. This was about twice as many large touring cars as were then being made in a like period by any other manufacturer in the world. In November, 1906, The White Company was organized with a capitalization of $2,500,000, and stockholders were given an opportunity to transfer their stock from the sewing machine company into that of the motor company at a fair valuation.

With characteristic modesty, Thomas H. White overlooked his share in its development and attributed the success of the new company entirely to his sons. He refused the presidency and delivered its progress entirely into their hands. It had now assumed important proportions, for along with the progress of the steam touring car the future of the commercial car had not been overlooked. From the very first a truck chassis had been under consideration, one such chassis having been turned out among the first five cars which were manufactured.

While the steam car was still moving triumphantly on its way White Company engineers were following the advances being made in the design of internal combustion engines and were preparing for the day when the gasoline car would "arrive." The first White gasoline truck appeared at the New York Automobile Show in 1910. It was a three-ton model, and was the result of ten years of patient study. Three other models, with capacities of two, three-quarters and five tons, followed shortly. Meanwhile, the motor truck market was developing rapidly.

By 1915 the general expansion of business necessitated further reorganization. The White Motor Company was organized with a capitalization of $16,000,000, which has since been increased to $25,-000,000. It succeeded to all the property of the White Company located at the factory and became the manufacturing organization, while the White Company retained all the branch office property and became a purely selling organization.

But although the old company was merged in the new one, it did not discard its old employees. This reminds me of an amusing incident. One of Walter White's strong individualities is his obstinate insistence that almost all men make good if they are doing the work they are fitted for and are properly handled. He works with his men to the limit, to bring out all there is in them.

"It took me long enough to find my niche," he says. "I'll give the other fellow the same chance."

As a result labor turnover is very low at the White plant, so low in fact that one day an inspector appeared from the Department of Labor.

"I think there must be some error in your figures," he said. "Your labor turnover is away below the usual figures for a plant of this size."

They opened the books. A careful search showed that the report was not only right, but that the turnover had been consistently low over a long period of years. The inspector was astonished. As he was leaving several of the workmen passed down the hallway.

"That man at the left has been with the Whites for forty-two years," said his guide, "and the man with him for over twenty."

"No wonder," said the inspector, "that they sent me down here to check up on turnover."

While the changes in organization were going on Walter White had not slackened his work on the sales end of the car. In the early days speed was the big talking point of the motor car and racing was a necessary adjunct. Webb Jay was racing under White colors and after repeatedly carrying them to victory he met with an accident. It left them without anyone to take his place.

"I was so close to that end of the business," said White, "that I did not look at it sanely. I was crazy to race that car, in two senses of the word.

"My first tryout was in the Vanderbilt Cup Race on Long Island, in 1907. I secured an imposing position, but it could not have been called exactly a success. But we got a lot of advertising for our car, just the same. After that I devoted most of my attention to hill climbing, in which I made a better record."

One hill climbing contest in which he was entered was at Wilkes-Barre, Pa. They did not close the entries until two days before the race. Three or four days before, White took his car out on a hill. Someone timed him. The night before the race was called he was barred from the free-for-all.

Such an injustice was not to be met quietly. After all, the big story is the fastest time; so White insisted that he be allowed to give an exhibition run. This was permitted and he beat the time record for the day. But still the committee refused him the cup, although the A. A. A. declared that he was entitled to it. Later on they admitted their error and sent him a duplicate.

His second race was run in Cleveland. Here he felt that he must either win or keep on going. He had a great desire to have his father see him come out ahead. At that time the Stearns was making a six-cylinder car. He went into that race for all there was in him and clipped six seconds off the time of the Stearns car, which held the record.

"There is one thing I never get over when I race," said White. "Once you are off you see nothing but the road and you have a maniacal desire to run over everybody and everything that comes in your way.

"Few people realize that when a car is going at such high speed it really is not under control, for it is in the air the best part of the time. To prove that this is so I took my car out once and raced it on a very dusty road. Afterwards we measured up its tracks. In one place it did not hit the ground for seventy feet."

After this race White decided he had had enough and would retire before he met with an accident, but like everyone else he stayed in just a little too long. The race was held in Cincinnati and the car turned over as it rounded the top of a hill, skidding on a cement cross-walk. White was underneath as the car rolled over at the curb, but he got out with a broken leg, which took a year to knit. That let him out of the racing field. It did not look like luck, but perhaps it was, for it forced Walter White into executive duties.

"But don't think you ever get over that racing urge," he flashed at me across his desk, "for you don't. Either it's in your blood or it isn't, and if it's there it stays."

Talking of sales he told me this story, which amply demonstrates the spirit which passes all through the organization.

"One of the things which we try not to withhold in

this organization is praise," said White. "It does not hurt anybody to be satisfied and it is often a great boost to the fellow who is doing the work. One of our salesmen in California happens to have the same spirit. Not long ago he was walking down the street when he caught sight of a scrupulously clean truck, whose driver was out of sight at the moment. Taking a card from his pocket he wrote these words on it and then tucked it into the steering wheel and went his way:

"'I don't know who owns this truck, but whoever does is lucky to have a man who takes care of it as you do. If you had a White and treated it this way it would last you twenty years.'

"Some little time later this same salesman was sent for by one of the large organizations in his district.

"'We have a man who is determined that we shall get him a White truck,' was the greeting he received. 'He is one of our best drivers and we are inclined to humor him. He tells us that some few months ago a White salesman stuck a card into his wheel. Are you the man?'

"The salesman pleaded guilty, and one more White truck moved out on the California road."

Why is it that investments in White trucks exceed $200,000,000 and that individual investments run as high as $3,000,000 or $4,000,000?

"If you want a man to have faith in you," said Walter C. White's father, "you must not betray his trust." The principle has stuck. When a man gets a good White truck it is not an accident. They are built neither by guess nor by luck, but by mathematics, science, and a system of testing which has no superior in the automobile field. When a White truck leaves the plant it carries with it the honor of the Whites.

O. D. F.

JOHN N. WILLYS

HOW is this for a come-back? From deficits aggregating almost $20,000,000 in 1920 and 1921 to profits approaching $20,000,000 in 1925.

From cash on hand of less than $300,000 in 1922 to some $20,000,000 at the end of three years.

From a balance sheet deficit of $43,000,000 to a profit and loss surplus of more than $25,000,000 in 1925.

From domination by bankers to domination by the management.

From a production of 96,623 cars in 1922 to a rate of over 215,000 a year.

From a low quotation of $4\frac{1}{2}$ for the common stock in 1922 to a quotation of 35, and from 24 to 124 for the preferred.

From no dividends on either preferred or common to 7 per cent. on the preferred, and prospects of a return to dividends for the common stock.

From an uncertain place in the industry to third in rank for the whole United States.

That is the record achieved by John N. Willys, head and backbone of the Willys-Overland Company.

This record is unique in the annals of American industry. Willys won his victory, not by any stock market manipulation, but by throwing off his coat, rolling up his sleeves and buckling down to the hardest of hard work both in the factory and in the selling field.

The post-war deflation, which brought so much ruin to industry and agriculture, badly shattered Willys-Overland and its affiliated enterprises. On top of this, Willys-Overland suffered from serious labor troubles which demoralized production and lowered the morale of dealers. Banking domination unnerved the executives, who scarcely knew who was who or what was what.

In short, Willys-Overland was beset with financial troubles, managerial troubles, labor troubles, distribution troubles. Its plight was so grave that at one time reports were circulated that the company would go out of business.

One man never lost faith in the outcome even when the clouds were blackest and the storm at its worst — John N. Willys.

"Learn to lose without squealing and to win without bragging," Willys once enunciated to me as a favorite maxim. Through all his troubles Willys never squealed.

While he was still hand-tied by bankers to whom his companies owed many millions of dollars, a prominent industrial leader complained bitterly that Wall Street "got" anybody it went after. "How about it?" I asked Willys. He replied:

"I don't believe that Wall Street ever sets out to 'get' any one. If Wall Street 'gets' any one it is because he has first put himself in a position where he lets Wall Street ' get ' him. I have no kick coming."

Few business men suffered more severely than John N. Willys when the bottom fell out of the post-war boom in 1920. Willys-Overland's financial troubles reached such a pass that in January, 1921, Willys asked that a banking committee be formed. Then followed months and months of talking and planning for refinancing. Finally, in the Fall, the bankers drafted a plan which, to quote Mr. Willys, " was satisfactory to the banking committee (as they were to be paid off), but I could not feel that it was fair to our stockholders."

" In the meantime," narrates Mr. Willys, " our sales department had to battle with the reports being constantly circulated that Willys-Overland would fail.

" Business in 1921 was bad, very bad, not only for us but for all automobile companies, as well as for other industrial institutions. I felt strongly that it was to our advantage to carry along negotiations without a decision as long as possible until the time would come when general business conditions would be better. I told one of our counsel that neither I nor any bankers could put Willys-Overland back on its feet until general business conditions became normal.

" The matter was carried along from October, 1921, to February, 1922, when the banking committee insisted that I go ahead and close the deal with the syndicate to refinance the company so that they could be paid off. I felt that this deal, while undoubtedly as good as any new interest could afford to offer, would ruin entirely the common stockholders' equity and probably the preferred. I arranged for the election of four Toledo business men to our board, men interested in having the business prosper for the sake of the city, the home of our main plants.

"After much wrangling, the bankers gave up the idea of forcing us to refinance and agreed to carry their loans for eighteen months, or until December 1, 1923.

"This eighteen months' extension gave us a breathing spell. The rumors that we were going to fail could be refuted by our salesmen. Our new board worked heroically to sell unnecessary property and turn slow accounts receivable into cash. These amounts when received were immediately paid on the indebtedness. At the same time, I put all my efforts on sales, and by July 1, 1922, had the factory filled with orders, so full that I felt that I could leave for sixty days to go abroad and get a much-needed rest and look into the affairs of our plant at Manchester, England.

"During my absence our leading competitors decided to make a big cut in the prices of their cars. I knew about this in advance and on my way to Europe I rushed a wireless to our general manager, telling the facts, followed by a letter advising our following their cut, which was to come on August 1. This letter was received in Toledo on July 24, but our general manager, seeing all the orders on hand, thought it would be foolish to lose the big profits we were making by following the cut. Our executive committee agreed that we needed the profits. So, against my advice, we stood pat.

"On my return on September 8, I found that our dealers had not been given proper information by our sales department, that orders had been cancelled, that our branches had become heavily stocked with cars, that all available space at the factory for storage was being used, and that business was practically at a standstill."

John Willys had other difficulties to wrestle with. Like many men of pioneering temperament, he had branched out vigorously and extensively while the sun was shining on his enterprises. In 1917, when every patriotic citizen had his mind on war work, Willys had organized the Willys Corporation as a holding company to facilitate expansion of his operations in various directions. Through this organization he had become interested in a number of automobile accessory concerns.

During the war boom Willys, among other things, secured control and energetically operated the Curtiss Aeroplane and Motor Corporation on a very broad scale; he bought control of the old-established Moline Plow Company, to develop it as a large producer of tractors; he was the leading factor in the Fisk Rubber Company, in the Electric Auto-Lite Company, and in various other projects.

I recall Mr. Willys saying to me one day during these boom times: "I am rounding out our activities so that we will produce on a large scale internal combustion machines for use in the air, on the surface of the ground, and in the ground — aeroplanes, automobiles, tractors. We are making great progress, also, towards becoming self-contained: I mean, we have planned to produce more and more of the parts and materials which go into our finished products."

Alas, the financial sunshine was to turn into financial storms. Willys, having launched enormous expansion, was caught before he had had time to put all his projects upon an impregnable basis. The consequence was that he had worries aplenty in addition to those connected with Willys-Overland. He had disposed of Curtiss Aeroplane in 1920 and, later, he got out of Moline Plow and several other concerns which had been sponsored by Willys Corporation.

Life for John N. Willys after the bursting of America's war boom was just one trouble after another. Everything seemed to go wrong — just as everything was going wrong with a multitude of other business men.

Had Willys been made of softer stuff, he would have been tempted to get from under and enjoy the competency he had earlier amassed. Instead of quitting the ship, he cleared the decks for action. He decided to leave his beautiful home on Long Island and his New York City house for the time being and to spend most of his time at the plant in Toledo and on the road, strengthening and licking into shape his sales organization throughout the continent. If he had for a time been taking life relatively easy, he now determined to work as he had never worked before.

And he did.

On his return from Europe he hastened to Toledo and began to carry out thorough-going house-cleaning. He became his own general manager, reorganized the running of the factory, overhauled the sales department and made many changes in the personnel. After a period of night-and-day studying at the plant, he began a series of strenuous trips to different territories to build up an efficient force of dealers. On some of these trips Willys hardly ever spent a night under a roof but always in trains, hastening from one town to another and saving time by doing his sleeping while traveling. The physical strain was terrific, but Willys never lost confidence in his ability to win out. This mental attitude enabled him to perform prodigious labor. With what result?

"At the end of one year," Mr. Willys relates, "the results of all our hard work, coupled with the general excellent automobile business that all companies enjoyed in 1923, enabled us to pay off our entire bank indebtedness of $17,357,500. On September 30, 1923, our statement showed no bank indebtedness, and our net profits for the year 1923 amounted to $13,034,032."

After feasting, famine. Whereas 1923 was the fattest year the automobile industry had ever known, 1924 proved rather a lean year. Even so, Willys-Overland continued to do relatively well. Great progress was made in fortifying the company's position both financially and physically. Very important improvements and additions were made to increase the productive capacity, a goal of 1,200 cars a day having been set.

Meanwhile, gratifying progress had been made in straightening out the affairs of the Willys Corporation, which was placed under the protection of the courts late in 1921. So effectively were things handled that creditors received payment in full.

Moreover, the lull in the automobile business during the second half of 1924 enabled Willys-Overland to perfect carefully-prepared plans for new models. At lunch with Mr. Willys one day in November, 1924, he remarked:

" If I were a betting man I would be willing to wager that 1925 will be by far the biggest year W. O. has ever had. Wait and see our new Willys-Overland Sixes and our new Willys-Knight Sixes at the Automobile Show in January. We *know* that they will be winners. We will give the public high-priced cars at the cost of low-priced cars."

Five months later, in April, 1925, Mr. Willys made this statement:

" Never before has the outlook for Willys-Overland been better. During March we built 5,200 Willys-Knight cars. We have now reached a production of 250 Overland Sixes per day and our output of Overland four-cylinder models has been nearly 600 cars a day, the majority being enclosed cars. Our dealers are already beginning to feel a brisk demand that presages a car shortage. We are employing nearly 20,000 men at our three plants in Toledo, Pontiac and Elmira —

14,000 men at Toledo and 3,000 each at the other two plants."

Three weeks later it was announced that April 20 brought a new production record for one day, with 1,193 Overland and Willys-Knight Sixes.

What of earnings?

In the first quarter of 1925 net profits, before Federal taxes, reached $3,171,466. That was encouraging; but it was nothing compared with what was to follow. April alone yielded more net than the total for the previous quarter, and for the full second quarter, net profits (before Federal taxes and special depreciations) were practically $6,000,000. The third quarter, usually the dullest of the year, surpassed the first three months, and total 1925 profits reached a new high record in the company's history.

In view of such earnings, it is not astonishing that the 30 per cent. back dividends on the preferred stock have been cleared up, thus paving the way for resumption of dividends on the common stock.

Naturally, the transformation in Willys-Overland's condition has attracted attention to the company's shares. On very active trading, the common has sold as high as 35 and the preferred, on which $1\frac{3}{4}$ per cent. quarterly is now being regularly paid, as high as 124.

Every man at the head of a large corporation must necessarily depend on the co-operation of others. The automobile industry agrees in testifying, however, that Willys-Overland's remarkable comeback can be credited almost wholly to one individual, John N. Willys.

What was Willys's training for the gigantic task he has so successfully carried out?

The story of John North Willys is picturesque, dramatic, peculiarly American. It is told at length in my book, "Men Who Are Making America." Only the main facts can be given here.

In the dark days of December, 1907, young Willys, then grubbing along as an automobile selling agent in Elmira, New York, became uneasy over the non-delivery of Overland cars, for which he had booked 500 orders. He hopped upon a train for Indianapolis, the Overland Company's headquarters, arrived on Saturday evening, and on Sunday morning was coolly told by the manager: "We are going into the hands of a receiver to-morrow morning."

"You are *not!*" Willys countered emphatically.

"We *are*," reiterated the manager. "Why, we paid some of our workmen by checks last night and we haven't enough money in the bank to meet them to-morrow morning."

"How much are you short?" asked Willys.

"About $350."

Indianapolis banks were paying out no real money in those memorable days. The town — like most of the United States — was on a scrip basis. But Willys meant to raise $350 by hook or by crook before the bank would open the next morning.

The interview occurred in the old Grand Hotel, where Mr. Willys had occasionally stopped. He walked boldly up to the hotel clerk.

"I want $350 cash before to-morrow morning," he informed the young man behind the desk.

"I wish you luck," came the laughing reply.

"You will have to get it for me," Willys told him.

"Swell chance!" came back the clerk, still thinking that Willys was joking.

Willys wrote out a check on a little bank in Wellsboro, Pa., for $350 and sternly told the clerk: "I must have cash for that before the bank here opens to-morrow morning." The clerk again laughed.

"Isn't the check good?" Willys demanded.

"I suppose it is, but where are you going to get $350 cash? I can't get a cent out of the bank."

There and then Willys planned a money-raising campaign. He told the clerk to freeze on to every dollar that came into the office, to gather up every cent collected in the restaurant, and to empty the barroom till.

"And don't cash another check for anybody until we get this money," Willys cautioned.

The proprietor, having been informed of the purpose for which the money was so urgently needed, entered into the spirit of the thing, and by midnight Willys was handed a mountain of silver dollars, half-dollars, quarters, dimes, and nickels, topped off with a thick layer of one-dollar bills and a sprinkling of twos, fives and tens.

Early next morning he planked the pile on the bank counter, to the credit of the Overland Company. The pay checks were duly met.

Within eight years John N. Willys, the saver of Overland, was offered $80,000,000 for his share of the company!

Of course, the mere raising of $350 hard cash that eventful Sunday did not bring the Overland concern back to life. It merely averted the threatened Monday morning crisis.

Instructing the company to stand off all creditors during the week, Willys hastened to Chicago and secured enough money there to meet the following Saturday's payroll. For five weeks he hurried and scurried from Indianapolis to Chicago and New York and back again, frantically trying to finance the company. The Overland plant then consisted merely of a sheet-iron shed 300 feet long by 80 feet wide, with a shopworn outfit of machinery and not enough material on hand to put out a single complete car. By frenzied scraping and cajoling, Willys procured sufficient materials to enable the company to finish enough cars to keep the working force together.

No banker would touch the concern. Creditors were clamoring for payment — the company owed $80,000 and hadn't $80 to its name.

Willys, however, was determined to stave off disaster. He had promised to supply 500 cars and had paid a substantial deposit to the company.

So effectively did Willys handle creditors that it actually took only $3,500 cash to swing the Overland's $80,000 debts and to start off a reorganized company without any financial burdens around its neck.

It was in January, 1908, that the reorganization was

accomplished. Willys became president, treasurer, general manager, sales manager, etc., etc. By September of the same year 465 cars had been made, sold (at $1,200 each), and delivered. And the company showed a net worth of $58,000. In the next twelve months, on this $58,000 capital, Willys manufactured and sold over 4,000 automobiles at a total price of $5,000,000 and cleaned up a net profit of over $1,000,000.

How John N. Willys first became interested in the automobile industry is a quaint story.

"I was standing looking out of a window in a skyscraper at Cleveland, Ohio, one day in 1899 when I noticed a thing on four wheels creeping along the street," Willys recalled to me. "No horse was attached to it. From where I was it looked exactly like a carriage. I immediately said to myself, 'That machine has all the bicycles in the country beaten hollow' — I was then in the bicycle business. I made up my mind that I would get into this new field at the first moment possible. I investigated and found that what I had seen was a Winton car.

"After having sold cars for a few years I made up my mind that the big money was to be made in making cars. But I had neither enough money nor manufacturing experience. Nor was I a mechanic. The best thing I could do, I concluded, was to form a large selling company, as I had done in bicycles, take the entire output of one or two companies, sell the cars at wholesale, and then graduate into the manufacturing end.

"So, in 1906, I formed the American Motor Car

Sales Company, with headquarters in Elmira, and undertook the sale of the whole output of the American and Overland companies, both in Indianapolis. I had to put up a big deposit, but I had lived economically and had saved some money. Before the panic started in October, 1907, our Sales Company had contracted to supply to dealers 500 Overland cars. I was anxious to branch out.

"Off I went to Indianapolis and signed a contract to distribute the Marion car. I was feeling quite happy on my way back to New York that evening when, phew! I picked up an evening paper and read that the Knickerbocker Trust Company had closed its doors and that pandemonium had broken out in New York.

"The Overland began to act suspiciously, and by the beginning of December things became so ominous that I decided to go to Indianapolis and investigate. You know what I discovered."

Up till then Mr. Willys had had a varied career. He was born, in 1873, in a place more noted for its natural beauty than as a gateway to millionairedom, Canandaigua, N. Y. From his earliest boyhood he was fond of making little business deals with his companions; he always had something in his pockets for sale. The first real initiative he showed was when, noticing how the reins were always falling down among horses' feet, he procured and sold a dozen little clamps for holding the reins. With the proceeds he bought two dozen and quickly disposed of them.

One of his chums was a lad who worked in a laundry,

and little Johnnie Willys became interested in this method of money-making. Before he was sixteen he had talked his parents into allowing him to buy, along with his young friend, a laundry at Seneca Falls, about thirty miles away. His parents hoped that a taste of roughing it in a laundry and in a boarding-house away from home would quickly cure him of his mania for business and drive him back home to his school books.

The budding knights of the wash-tub and the ironing-board discovered they had been "stuck." However, they buckled down to business with grim determination.

At the end of a year, having succeeded in putting the laundry on a paying basis, they sold out with a net profit of $100 each.

By this time Willys regretted he had not had more education. He returned home with the intention of working his way through college and becoming a lawyer. He was getting along quite well with his studies and working in a law office when his father died. Young Willys had to give up his college aspirations.

Bicycles were beginning to make their appearance, and he thought he saw in them a profitable outlet for his ingenuity as a salesman. With the $100 he had cleaned up on the laundry, he bought a sample bicycle, the "New Mail," and was duly authorized as a local agent for the manufacturers. By the time he was nineteen he had organized a Sales Company, opened a store, established a repair shop in the rear, and prospered so much that by and by he opened a larger establishment in Canandaigua's main street.

"I surely was going on the high gear," Mr. Willys remarked in discussing his youthful experiences. "I could sell any number of bicycles; but I made the mistake of taking everybody to be honest, just as I was. I found it was one thing to sell bicycles and another thing to collect the money. It needed only the upheaval caused by the free silver rumpus of 1896 to bowl me over. That was one of the best things that ever happened to me. It taught me a lesson. It put business sense into my head."

Taking a job as a traveling salesman with the Boston Woven Hose & Rubber Company, he worked hard and saved money in preparation for reentering business on his own account. Among his customers was the Elmira Arms Company, a sporting goods store which had bankrupted four proprietors in succession. Willys bought it at a bargain and installed a manager. Then the Woven Hose Company failed. Willys promptly took personal hold of his store, made a specialty of bicycles, became a wholesale distributor, and built up a business of half-a-million a year — not a mean record for a man of twenty-seven.

After he entered the automobile manufacturing field, Willys worked from seven in the morning to midnight daily for several years — until the doctors told him he must either drop everything and go pleasure-seeking in Europe or be prepared to become an inmate of a sanitarium. He was automobiling in France along with

Mrs. Willys and their only child (a daughter) when the war broke out and his limousine was at once commandeered. But he made up for it by booking orders for a few thousand motor trucks from the Allies before he left Europe!

During the war Willys became the American Navy's chief supplier of aircraft and had everything geared up to become the country's largest producer of airships when the armistice came. His eventful experiences since then have already been outlined.

Just as Willys learned " to lose without squealing," so he has learned " to win without bragging."

B. C. F.